FROM THE ASHES

The Rise of the University of Washington Volleyball Program

Frank Zaccari

TABLE OF CONTENTS

* * *

From the Ashes

DEDICATION

* * *

To Jim and Margaret McLaughlin, you are the architects of this truly amazing success story. What you accomplished is not just a blueprint for volleyball or even an athletic program. Every type of business, organization, non profit and family can benefit from the processes, procedures, philosophies, and steadfast commitment to principles that you brought to the University of Washington. Your attention to detail is as legendary as your now-famous sayings "there are no small things" and "improve on something every day." I attribute much of my success when I changed careers at age fifty to the things I heard you say. Thank you for the pleasure of watching your teams play at the highest level, and thank you even more for your support and friendship.

To Sanja Tomasevic, thank you for coming to the University of Washington and for all your insight for this book. This program started with your talent; your passion; your drive; and your goal to be on the court when UW won its first national title. Without you, this story does not happen in four years. You will forever be the cornerstone of this program.

To the University of Washington players and staff during the Jim McLaughlin era, this tremendous success could not have happened without you. You made the plays, you put in the hard work, and you made yourselves great. We, your fans, simply enjoyed the fruits of your labor.

For every copy of this book that is sold, $1 will be donated to the University of Washington volleyball program. Go Huskies!

Chapter 1

THIS CAN'T BE RIGHT

* * *

My name is Frank Zaccari. I started watching college volleyball about 1992. My daughter Stephanie was four, and Sara wasn't even born yet. I started by bringing them to see Sacramento State play in the terrible little gym on the Sac State campus. High schools, for that matter, many junior high schools, had better facilities, but I wanted my daughters to see women as active participants, not just spectators. I wanted them to see that women can be anything if they set their mind to it and are willing to put in the effort. The fact that Sac State, under now Hall of Fame Coach Debby Colberg, was a good program and we found ourselves enjoying volleyball was a bonus.

After Sara was born, we started going to every Sac State home match. My daughters and I would go to the far end of the gym, as far away as we could from everyone else. This allowed my girls to play on the bleachers and in the corner of the gym without bothering anyone. It also allowed me to watch the games. As long as I bought my daughters Skittles, Sunbursts, popcorn, and a root beer every game, they were happy. Their mother wasn't too crazy about what I was feeding them—but like I told her, "If you don't like what I give them, then come to the games with us and you can buy them whatever you want." Because I travelled so much for work, their mother really enjoyed having a free night, so she didn't complain too much about my dietary selections.

At first we didn't really understand the game. I had played in very recreational league, pre-children, when I lived and worked in South Carolina. It wasn't highly competitive. It was more of a "play the game, then drink beer" league. We didn't know many of the rules, and even less about strategy and rotations—but we did enjoy watching little Sac State play. About 1998, I was visiting my brother Steve who was living in Phoenix after he had been paralyzed in a car accident. Steve was a big booster of the Arizona State (ASU) women's athletics. Steve took me to an ASU vs. Stanford volleyball match. This level of volleyball was far superior to anything I had ever seen. The women were so much taller, stronger, and more athletic than Sac State and the teams in the Big Sky conference. My brother quickly educated me that the PAC-10 was far and away the best volleyball league in the nation. Programs like UCLA, University of Southern California (USC), Stanford, ASU, and University of Arizona were always ranked in the Top 10. Stanford, UCLA, or USC was often in the Final Four. More times than not, a PAC-10 school won the national title. For me, watching ASU and Stanford was like an epiphany. The game was so fast. The athletes were so good. I was awestruck. I had to see more. Unfortunately for me, the nearest PAC-10 schools were Stanford and Cal, both over two hours from Sacramento if traffic is good—and traffic is never good. As any parent with ten- and five-year-old daughters will tell you, there is *no way* you are going to drive two hours each way to watch a volleyball game unless one of the players is a family member. So my PAC-10 volleyball was limited to visiting my brother during volleyball season. Few if any PAC-10 teams had ever come to play at Sac State. The Big Sky conference was light years away from competing with the PAC-10.

In 1999, the University of Washington (UW) Huskies came to Sacramento to play Sac State. The game was on a Friday night. I figured it was basically a warm-up game, since UW was scheduled to play the University of Pacific (UOP), a nationally ranked program at that time, the next night in Stockton. I packed up my daughters and told them we are going to see a PAC-10 team play. I told them we are going to see bigger, stronger, and faster players. My daughters asked, "So is Sac State going to lose?" I said they probably would because the PAC-10 schools usually get the more gifted players. UW came onto the court, and they looked impressive. They were tall, lean, appeared well conditioned. The Sac State team looked like lambs going to the

slaughter. Then the match began. Sac State setter Maureen Raf-
ferty kept the Huskies off balance, and outside hitters Angela
Lewis and Carissa Buie pounded kill after kill. I was shocked. In
1999 the games went to 15 points, you could only score when
you served, and it was a best-of-five format. Sac State won all
three games by the amazing scores of 15-6, 15-5, and 15-8. The
University of Washington, a PAC-10 program, could only score a
grand total of 19 points in three games against a Big Sky team. I
could not believe what I just saw. I thought, "This can't be right.
Is Sac State really that good? Is UW really that bad?" Then ratio-
nalizations started. Maybe Sac State was more fired up to play
against a PAC-10 team on their home court. Maybe Sac State
played the game of their lives. Maybe UW took Sac State too
lightly because they were focused on UOP the next night. My
daughters were thrilled, since Angela Lewis and Carissa Buie
were their two favorite players. They were like the little boy "Still-
well Angel" in the movie *A League of Their Own* as they danced
on the floor, holding their noses, pointing at UW, and singing,
"You're gonna lose, you stink." I just could not believe UW was
that bad. So the next night I packed up my daughters and we
drove forty miles to Stockton to watch UW play UOP. Surely, UW
would be fired up and better prepared to take on the highly
ranked UOP Tigers. After the embarrassing loss to Sac State, I
figured UW would be ready to exact some revenge. I was wrong.
UOP swept the Huskies in three straight games, 15-4, 15-8, 15-5.
UW scored only 17 points in three games. Now let's give some
credit to Sac State and UOP. Sac State beat four PAC-10 teams
that season, Washington, Oregon State, Arizona, and Washington State. No PAC-10 teams wanted to schedule Debby Colberg
and her Sac State Hornets after that season. In 1999, Sac State
made it to the second round of the NCAA tournament, where,
ironically, they lost to UOP.

I called my brother Steve and told him what I had just
seen. Then I asked if he had seen UW play. He told me UW was
pretty good a few years back when they had Angela Branson,
Markare Desilets, Laurie Wetzel, and Leslie Tuiasosopo. The program had fallen on very bad times, but he didn't know why.

He said, "The best thing about UW is they are two wins per year for ASU."

I kept an eye on the Washington team the rest of the season. They finished in eighth place in the PAC-10 with a record of 8-18. As someone who made a very good living turning around failing high-tech companies, I couldn't help thinking that UW volleyball was in need of a turn-around plan. I wondered if the business principles and practices I used to turn companies around could work for an athletic team or program. How could a program that represented one of the finest universities in the nation, with the loyal alumni and donors in Seattle, with money coming from one of the best football programs in the nation, and with facilities equal to the best programs in the nation, play so poorly?

Chapter 2

UW VOLLEYBALL, UP CLOSE AND PERSONAL

* * *

I didn't spend a great deal of time thinking about how to turn-around the UW volleyball program. While I had travelled to Seattle many times in my high-tech life, I never had any desire to move to the Northwest. In late 1999 that all changed.

I was trying to arrange a way to move to Denver. The company I was running had an office in Denver, and we were developing a love for the city. I took my wife on a few trips to Denver, and we took a family vacation one summer to Keystone. Even the snow didn't bother me, which is a big deal for someone who grew up in Buffalo, New York. Before we could make the necessary connections and arrangements for a move to Denver, I received a call asking me to consider a job in Seattle with a company named Computech Systems. The position was vice president of sales and marketing. At this point I was not interested in another vice president position. The recruiter and the company's chief executive officer were persistent. They said, "Take a trip up here and let's talk. There is no harm in talking." So I took a quick trip to Seattle. I met with the CEO, president, chief financial officer, and director of technical services. Nice guys—but I was really not interested in relocating my family for a lateral move. I flew back home thinking I wouldn't take the job. A few days later, I get a call from the chairman of the board, who asked me to come back and meet with the board of directors. I thought, "This is a pretty strange process for hiring a VP of sales." I told him I really didn't see the point. He told me, "We are planning to start a dot-com business, and the current CEO will leave to run the dot-com company. We want to meet with you to discuss you becoming the president and CEO. We'll fly you and your wife up on Thursday. You meet with the board Friday morning, and then

you and your wife spend the weekend in Seattle. We will schedule her for a spa session at the Woodmark Inn Friday morning
so we can talk." I talked about it with my wife, and we decided,
what the hell, a free weekend in Seattle—and all I had to do was
meet with some people from 8 to 10 Friday morning.

The Woodmark Inn is a great place. It is right on Lake Washington at Carillion Point. Across the lake is the University of Washington campus. Down the street are some great restaurants in
Kirkland, and a few miles away is downtown Seattle. We have
all heard the stories about the Seattle rain, but that weekend in
November it was beautiful. No rain at all. The sun was out during the day. The sky was a shade of blue I had never seen before.
Mount Rainier looked close enough to touch. We ate at Daniel's
Broiler and Duke's (greatest clam chowder in the world). We had
a great weekend together. Sunday morning the chairman of the
board called the hotel and said they would fax the first draft of
an offer to our house Monday morning. The offer was outstanding. Complete control of the day to day operations. Money was
far more than we were making. My concern was the company
had been losing over $400,000 per year for the last four years. Its
revenue stream was not adequate to continue to absorb such
large losses. I wasn't sure I could turn this one around. I thought
it might be a liquidation, not a turn-around. I decided to take
the job. I would move to Seattle in January alone. I would rent
an apartment. The family would stay in Sacramento until the
school year ended in June. This way, if I didn't believe I could save
the company after six months, we wouldn't have to go through
the relocation issue. So I moved up to Seattle. I would go home
two weekends a month. The family would come to Seattle one
weekend, and one weekend neither would travel.

I plowed right into the job. The place was a mess. The financial situation was terrible. Expenses were way out of line; the
company had a huge loan to service, revenue was down, and it
had nearly $300,000 in obsolete inventory. One night the chair-
man of the board came into my office about 7:30. He asked,
"How are things going?"

I told him, "You need to tell me what you haven't told me."

He said, "Like what?"

I said, "Like what the $1 million loan was actually used to finance."

"It was just for day-to-day operations," he said.

My eyes widened as I leaned forward and said, "It is poor fiscal management to take on long-term debt for short-term expenditures." He said he agreed and that was why I was there.

I told him, "This place is in terrible condition, and it will take over one year to get rid of most of the bad contracts and inventory. I will only be evaluated on operating profit/loss, since I did not incur the huge debt or make the other poor decisions."

He said that was fair and the board was not expecting an instant miracle. With that settled, I went to work changing the personnel, the product mix, receiving and testing procedures, and inventory processing, and I started to change the culture. It was a daunting challenge—but it was exhilarating.

It was six or seven months before I even thought about the UW volleyball program. Finally I contacted the program in late June or early July 2000. I told the team administrator about my involvement with Sacramento State and asked about their booster group. She sounded very excited as she told me, "We are a member of the PAC-10, which is the best volleyball conference in the world."

I laughed and told her, "I know that much. Tell me more about the program."

"Well, let me tell you, our head coach is Bill Neville, who was the head coach of the 1972 and 1976 Canadian men's Olympic teams. He was an assistant coach on the 1984 U.S. men's gold medal Olympic team. Bill has been with us since 1991, and we have an excellent team." I was impressed with the energy and excitement in her voice.

"That is an impressive resume, but what happened the last two years?" I asked.

"We made the Sweet 16 in 1997, so we are rebuilding and making great progress," was the reply.

Having grown up in New York, I sometimes find myself reverting to back to my New York roots. "You still have a very long way to go. I saw you lose to Sacramento State last year. A PAC-10 team should never lose to a Big Sky team, ever."

She just laughed and said, "I will set up a lunch with you and Coach Neville."

The lunch was set early the next week at The Ram, a well known UW hangout. Coach Neville told me, "We have a very active booster group that is called POINT! HUSKIES! Every time the team scores a point, the crowd yells out 'POINT! HUSKIES!,' hence the name. People who donate at least $500 are given special seating." He asked, "Can you donate at least $500?" I assured him I could. He continued to explain that there were fifteen to twenty people who met every two weeks to discuss ways to help raise money and support the program.

I started going to the meetings, but didn't find them to be very productive. Most of the meetings consisted of the coach telling stories about the USA men's team that won a gold medal. The stories were interesting, but we weren't accomplishing much for the program. The fundraisers were what people did in high school, things like raffles, bake sales, car washes. To make matters worse, this group wanted the players to work the events. I thought to myself, "This is ridiculous. These are scholarship athletes going to a leading academic university. The demands on the players' time for training, practice, games, and classes were overwhelming. Then this group wanted to take what little free time they had to walk to all the tailgate parties before football games and sell raffle tickets. While all the booster members were nice people and their hearts were in the right place, very little was happening to help improve the program or raise any money.

The 2000 team was terrible. They dropped from eighth place to last in the PAC-10. I made my donation, so my family had preferred sitting, which was nice, but most of the matches were brutal. The first PAC-10 home game was against ASU. Of course, my brother called me to let me know ASU was loaded and fully expected to make short work of the Huskies. He was right. As we entered the arena, we were given a sign with the words POINT! HUSKIES! and the instructions when the Huskies score a point to hold up the sign and yell POINT! HUSKIES! My daughters were still fairly young, so they were very excited. If memory serves me right, ASU scored the first 10 points. My daughters kept waiting for the opportunity to jump up, hold up their sign, and yell—but it wasn't happening. Finally after about the ninth straight point, my oldest daughter took out a pen and wrote the letters N-O on the sign. When ASU scored its next point, she jumped up, held up her modified sign, and yelled, "NO POINT! HUSKIES!" Everyone around us laughed. It was funny—sad, but funny. ASU won the first game 15-1. Games two and three weren't much better. ASU won them 15-10 and 15-6. It was going to be that type of year for UW. The team only won two matches in the PAC-10. Both wins went the full five sets, but the Huskies prevailed against Oregon and Oregon State. As bad as the team was in 1999 when we saw them play Sac State and UOP, this team was worse. You could see the frustration growing in Coach Neville throughout the year, and he struggled to find the right mix and combination of players. To make matters worse there was major drama between the players. It seemed to me the coaches spent more time playing Dr. Phil, trying to control the drama and division in the locker room, than actually coaching volleyball. This was particularly frustrating for Coach Neville, who had proven over many years that he was and is an excellent volleyball coach. Here in 2000, the man who had success everywhere he went, including an Olympic gold medal, was now the captain of the *Titanic*. This was the third consecutive losing season coming after his greatest season in 1997. In the past three seasons, the Huskies had finished seventh, eighth, and tenth in the PAC-10. Attendance was down. The players, most of whom were giving everything they had, were frustrated and depressed with the season. The in-state rival Washington State Cougars came to Seattle and beat the Huskies 15-2, 15-7, 15-13, and, to add insult to injury, the Cougars had more fans that stood and sang their victory song on our court. Everyone was happy when the season ended. There was so much drama that instead of the usual end-of-the-season team banquet, the decision was made to take the team, parents, and a few donors bowling. Some of the players didn't even attend. I remember thinking, "Wow, some-thing has to happen before next season." To me there was hope for the future. Allison Richardson and Lisa Underhill would be back for one more season. Paige Benjamin and Gretchen Maurer had two more seasons. It was a good nucleus to build upon.

＊ ＊ ＊

The booster meetings continued to be counterproductive. I scheduled a meeting with Coach Neville and the team admin-istrator in early March to discuss some ideas for the program. In scheduling the meeting, I told them, "I am very disappointed with the lack of any real action or activity with the booster group. Hopefully we can brainstorm some ideas."

I did some research before the meeting. It appeared vol-leyball started at UW in 1974. The program had five coaches from 1974 through 1990. The teams did fairly well from 1974 to 1990, winning 359 matches and losing 246. The program made to the AIAW Tournament in 1979 and 1980. The AIAW was the precursor to the NCAA Tournament. UW had made the NCAA Tournament in 1986, 1988, and 1989. They made it to the sec-ond round of the tournament in 1988. The 1989 team finished in second place in the PAC-10, number 10 in the nation, and made the NCAA Tournament. These results are not bad. Granted, they aren't great, but they are not bad. Coach Neville took over part way through the 1991 season through 2000. The team had 135 wins and 131 losses. He led UW to the second round of the NCAA Tournament in 1994 and 1996. In 1997 the team made it to the Sweet 16. That is a very good four-year run. It included three of the university's six NCAA Tournament appearances. Coach Nev-ille had 72 of its 135 wins in that four-year span and developed two All-Americans, Angela Bransom in 1996 and Makare Desi-lets in 1997. Up to 1997 there had only been four All-Americans total. In 1998, 1999, and 2000, the program had deteriorated, winning 25 matches while losing 52. It was the last three years I wanted to discuss.

We had our meeting at The Ram. Since I called for the meeting, I started off by thanking them for their time. Then I said, "Coach, from 1994 through 1997, the program was very good. My guess is graduation took a big toll after 1997, but it would seem to me that given the success, recruiting would have improved."

"Graduation hit us pretty hard in '96 and '97," he said. "We lost two All-Americans and our setter. After the 1996 season we tried to recruit the 'elite players' in the country. We were in the running for a couple of them, but they went elsewhere. I probably didn't have as good of a Plan B for recruiting as I would have liked. That's all water under the bridge."

I said, "It is what it is. What I really wanted to talk about are some ideas for POINT! HUSKIES! It seems to me we are relying too much on the car-raffle program that Barbara Hedges (the athletic director) started and far too much on the players driving the actual fundraising. What I suggest is we contact donors that could give $5,000 or more directly and set up one-on-one meetings to present the direction of the program and how we plan to get back to the Sweet 16. There must be a database of donors somewhere."

The team administrator said, "We haven't been very diligent in keeping the database current. What happened is we started adding many people who probably shouldn't be on the list. For example, team bus drivers and other people who probably can't or won't make a donation. So the list isn't of much value."

"Okay, then, I suggest we do a purge on the list. How about at the next POINT! HUSKIES! meeting, we all go through the list. I suggest we keep the people that someone knows during the first pass, and then start listing names of people they know who may be interested in volleyball and have the means to make a donation."

"There are some issues with that," said Coach Neville. "The athletic department doesn't want the small-revenue sports to be hitting up the big donors directly. They need the big donors for football and men's basketball."

"I'm not suggesting we approach people who give $100,000 or more. What is the most the program has raised with the current activities?"

"Somewhere around $7,000," was the response.

"So the raffle program where the players actually walk around to tailgate parties at the football games and the basketball tip-off luncheon and work a barbeque generates this money. Is that correct?"

"Pretty much," said Coach Neville. "Donors like interacting with the players. It helps them build a connection with the players."

"Frank, we are a minor-revenue sport," the administrator added. "We are limited to what we can do."

I was starting to get frustrated but asked them both to please elaborate.

The administrator said "Well, for example, we can't approach large companies directly because the athletic department and/or the school have a contract with them. We can't put up sponsors for volleyball-only signs in the arena for the same reason. We can't sell apparel because another group has the rights. We can't have donors work concessions stands because there is a contract with Marriott."

I took a deep breath, then said, "I do understand there are limitation on what can be done; however, I am not suggesting we do monumental events. I suggest that instead of talking about what we can't do, let's see if we can identify things we can do. For example, just talking to twenty-five donors who can give just $500 each is $12,500. That is more than you have been raising and it doesn't wear out the players. It seems to me the players have enough demands on their time between practice, games, travel, and school. We have to do or try something different. The members of POINT! HUSKIES! need to be more active and more accountable to help generate some funds and promote the program."

"Things like this have been tried in the past. The members all have full-time jobs, lives, and family commitments. Most of them don't have the time" was the response.

I was starting to get annoyed. It was like talking to most of the staff at Computech. What they were doing wasn't working, but they were not willing to try anything new. Finally, I said, "Okay, then, how about changing the guidelines for POINT! HUSKIES!? If you want to be a member of the board, then you have to bring some fundraising ideas to the party and help drive the events. I am talking about working the front doors at the matches. I suggest something like we raffle off a signed volleyball at every match. As people come in, POINT! HUSKIES! members hand them the game day flyer and ask them to fill out a raffle card. The card will have their name, address, e-mail, phone number, and name of their favorite Husky. We can put a line on the card that says we may be contacting you regarding future volleyball events. We collect the cards *before* the match begins, than we draw one name. The winner will be announced at the break. We give them the signed volleyball and they get their picture taken with their favorite player after the match. We give the cards to the database person, and we start building a list with people that we know have actually attended a match."

Once again the suggestion was rejected. "The marketing department handles the pregame things."

I took another deep breath, rubbed my forehead, and said, "Why don't I write up a plan that we all can review? I believe we have to become more proactive. If the decision is to keep the status quo, then there is no reason for me to stay with the program. We have to generate some excitement. When Washington State came here, they had more fans and were more vocal than our fans. This is our in-state rival and they outdraw us at our place."

The meeting ended with the administrator saying "Frank, we are open to ideas, but you have to understand, most of the group has been together for several years. You are the new guy, and you bring new energy and ideas which we need, but they have to be agreed to by the other members. Write up your plan and we will go through it and rework it, then present it to the group."

I thanked them for their time and headed back to my office. On the drive I came to the realization that the similarities between companies in crisis and the volleyball program were strikingly similar. Both were failing but were unwilling or unable to try new approaches. Both became very defensive when a new person came in and tried to initiate change. Both had the majority of the staff say they were open to hearing the new plan but would not make a real effort to help execute it. Both would rather stand on the sidelines and watch the new plan fail, then say, "I knew it wouldn't work." The pastor at a church I belonged to back in Sacramento once told me, "The big difference between a business and a volunteer organization is you can fire people in a business. In a volunteer organization you are pretty much stuck with who you have." I told him, "It may be easier to fire people in a business, but if the leader of a largely volunteer organization does not change or remove or encourage some people to leave, then that leader will not have an organization for very long."

Chapter 3

TURN-AROUND RULE #1—FIND THE RIGHT LEADER

* * *

I spent most of April and May focused on my business. Computech made a small operating profit the first year. We kept our heads down and focused on making cuts, enhancing efficiency and effectiveness of our processing, and expanding our product mix. The profit margins on previously owned computer hardware continued to drop. So it was either continue to significantly increase our volume or find a product or service that generated better margins. I spun out a service-based company with the hopes of securing higher profit service business to our customers who purchased the equipment. After a few bumpy months, the service company started to turn a real profit.

I continued to think about what type of business plan to propose to Coach Neville. How much of what I was doing in the business world would apply to the volleyball program? I decided to make a list of the steps I followed in the business world. I found ten steps or rules or guidelines or principles (call them what you want) that had worked for me in successfully turning around six different organizations. The more I thought about my list, the more I was convinced they would work with any type of business or organization. My ten rules are as follows:

1. Everything starts with having the right leader.
2. The leader must clearly articulate his/her vision.
3. The leader must inspire people to believe.
4. The leader must clearly define what he or she wants to do and what pieces he or she needs to get there.

5. The leader must select the right people and put them in the best position to succeed.
6. The leader must focus on the details and training. Make sure everyone knows not only what to do but how and why to do it.
7. The leader must insist that everything is documented. The organization must be able to operate without key people present.
8. The leader must constantly review all aspects of the operation and make adjustments as needed to stay on course.
9. The leader must continue to bring in people that are better than the ones already in place.
10. The leader cannot lose sight of the goal.

In late June I started to define how these rules would apply to UW volleyball. Before the plan was complete, I learned that Coach Neville had resigned in mid-July. The team was due to arrive for the start of training camp in three weeks and the head coach had just resigned. The POINT! HUSKIES! board met to see what, if anything, we should do. The meeting didn't accomplish much. Most of the time was spent speculating about why Coach Neville resigned and what actions Athletic Director Barbara Hedges could take. Since none of us in the room had any role in the decision-making process, what we thought or said had no real value. I did call Coach Neville to see how he was doing. He told me he was fine and was okay with his decision. He said no one pushed him out or asked him to leave. Then he told me, "Frank, I have been doing this for so long that I am probably burned out and need a break."

"Believe me, Coach; I know exactly how you feel. I burned out a few years ago myself. I took nearly a year off to get back in touch with my family and try to decide what I wanted to do. You are a good man and have done a great deal for volleyball. Take some time for you."

"That's my plan," was his response.

"Do you think Barbara Hedges has someone in mind, or do you think she will promote one of your assistants given that the team will be here in a couple of weeks?"

"Barbara always has someone in mind. She'll find someone."

* * *

Barbara Hedges was in Hawaii when she received the call that Coach Neville had resigned. After Barbara stopped venting, the senior associate who made the call said, "So what is the plan? The team will be here on August 10 and we have *no coach*."

Barbara answered, "I know a guy."

Exasperated, the senior associate yelled. "Barbara, everyone knows a guy. How are we going to get a guy, get him hired, moved out here, and ready to start practice in three weeks?"

"Don't worry. I know a guy."

"We better get a plan B and C just in case, Barbara. I will talk to the assistants and get some input from them."

"I'm going to call the guy right now. This is right guy for the job. I know him. He will take this job."

* * *

Twenty minutes later, Jim McLaughlin's cell phone rings. He was driving with longtime mentor Carl McGowan to a coaching clinic they were conducting. Jim's version of the call was something like this:

"Jim, this is Barbara Hedges. Congratulations on your success at Kansas State. Making it to the Sweet 16 had to be a thrill."

"What can I do for you, Barbara?"

"As you know, Bill Neville resigned, and I am looking for someone with a proven track record to make this program a national power."

"Barbara, every team in the country starts practice in three weeks. People with proven resumes are getting ready to meet their teams. I can suggest a couple of people from USA Volleyball."

"Jim, I am calling you because I want you. You have done a great job at K-State, but you belong back in the PAC-10, where you have a chance to win a national title with a women's program, so you can put that trophy next to your USC men's national title."

"Barbara, I can't leave now. My team arrives in three weeks. I will check with some people and have them call you."

"Jim, talk to your wife. I want you to fly out to Seattle this weekend so we can talk. You belong in the PAC-10. If you still say no, you and your lovely wife will have a weekend in Seattle. It is beautiful here in Seattle right now. I'll have plane tickets waiting for you. Talk to Margaret and call me back."

"Goodbye, Barbara."

Jim looked over at Carl, who asked, "That was Barbara Hedges and she offered you the job at Washington, didn't she?"

"Yeah, she said she wants to talk."

"Take the job, Jim."

"Carl, I can't take the job. My team arrives in three weeks. We can't pull this together in three weeks."

"Jim, take the job. Your assistant is ready to become a head coach. If you stay at K-State, your assistant will be gone next year anyway. You have done a great job at K-State, but they don't have the resources or the drawing power to win the national title. Washington has great facilities. They have great fans and donors. They have money. Hell, their football team generates more money than most small countries. Seattle is one of the greatest cities in the country. They have great schools for your kids. Seattle doesn't get snow and cold like Kansas. Jim, it's the PAC-10, the best volleyball conference in the world. Jim, are you crazy? Take the job."

"She didn't actually offer the job."

"Call Barbara back today. Get on a plane and talk. Remember when you left the USC men's program. No one would hire you as a head coach because they said, 'Women can't play the men's style of volleyball. Women don't have the strength or the speed.'

We both told them, 'They aren't playing against men.' Now you have proven that women can play the men's style at Notre Dame and at K-State. You got K-State to the Sweet 16. You belong in the PAC-10. You can build a national power in Washington and win a few national titles. You have proven that women can play the men's game. It's time to take your program to the best conference in the country."

Jim called his wife, Margaret, and they made the flight to Seattle. For those of you who don't know Barbara Hedges, she is one of the most passionate and persuasive people in the world. She loved the University of Washington and wanted all of her teams to compete for national championships every season. Jim and Barbara had history. Barbara was the assistant AD at USC when Jim coached the men's team. He had won the national title and played in the national title game the next season. This was not a knee-jerk reaction. She knew Jim was the right person.

On August 1, 2001, Barbara Hedges announced her new volleyball coach, Jim McLaughlin. The press release was as follows:

McLaughlin brings 11 years of head coaching experience

August 1, 2001

SEATTLE—Jim McLaughlin, head coach at Kansas State University for the past four seasons, has been named head women's volleyball coach at the University of Washington, UW athletic director Barbara Hedges announced today. McLaughlin, who led the USC men's volleyball team to the 1990 NCAA title, becomes the seventh head coach in school history.

"I just want to thank Barbara and the University of Washington for the opportunity to come and coach at such an outstanding institution," McLaughlin said. "I chose to come to Washington, because of the people and the professionalism that they showed when I was there.

"The University of Washington has a great academic reputation and the success of the athletic department has been phenomenal. As a family, we are excited to be coming to Seattle."

McLaughlin replaces former head coach Bill Neville who announced his retirement on July 17, after ten years at Washington.

"We are thrilled to have the McLaughlin's join the Husky family," Hedges said. "Jim was clearly our top candidate and he brings exceptional credentials as well as championship experience to the Washington volleyball program."

McLaughlin spent the last four seasons building the Kansas State women's volleyball program into a national power, compiling an 82-43 record and taking the Wildcats to four consecutive NCAA tournament appearances. Last season, McLaughlin led Kansas State to a 22-9 record, a program-best number sixteen national ranking, and its first-ever trip to the NCAA Sweet 16.

During his tenure at Kansas State, two Wildcats earned All-America honors, seven were named to the All-Big 12 first team, and fifteen garnered first-team academic all-conference accolades. McLaughlin also was honored as the 1999 Big 12 conference coach of the year.

Prior to a one-year stint as an assistant at Notre Dame in 1996, McLaughlin was the head men's coach at the University of Southern California for seven seasons, leading the Trojans to the NCAA title in 1990 (his first season as head coach) and a runner-up finish a year later. While at USC, McLaughlin's teams were ranked in the top ten five times, while fifteen players earned All-America accolades, led by two-time national player of the year, Bryan Ivie.

McLaughlin's volleyball career began as a player, first at Santa Monica Junior College (1980-81) and later at his alma mater, UC Santa Barbara (1982-83), where he was the Gauchos' starting setter for two seasons, earning honorable mention All-America honors as a senior.

After two years as a student assistant coach for both the UCSB men's and women's squads, McLaughlin became an assistant at Pepperdine University (1986-89) where he helped coach the Waves to the 1986 NCAA men's title.

The Malibu, Calif., native also has had experience coaching on the international level as a three-time head coach at the World University Games, in addition to being a consultant for the U.S. Men's Olympic teams in both 1992 and 1996.

Well, Coach Neville was right: Barbara had someone in mind, and on paper it appears she hit it out of the park.

I met with a few of the POINT! HUSKIES! board members at The Ram to see if anyone knew Jim McLaughlin. No one had first-hand knowledge on him, but he had an incredible set of credentials. The man knew how to win. He was a national champion as an assistant and head coach in men's volleyball. Plus, he made Kansas State a top-twenty program. I remember saying, "If this guy made Kansas State in Manhattan, Kansas, a national power, he knows what he is doing."

One of the board members asked, "Why do you say that?"

"Because have you ever been to Manhattan, Kansas? He was able to either get high-caliber players to come to Manhattan, Kansas, not an easy feat, or he was able to train kids from Kansas, not exactly a hot bed for volleyball talent, to become a top-twenty team. Either way, the man can coach."

* * *

The next few weeks became a whirlwind for the McLaughlin family. They had to sell a house in Kansas; find a place in Seattle; move two preschool children; hire a coaching staff; and get ready to meet the team, the vast majority of whom Jim had never met or seen play. Of course, there was no pressure, but all this had to be done in nine days. Oh, and by the way, he had to have the team ready to play in a preseason tournament against Brigham Young and Texas, who were both nationally ranked, as well as Purdue at the end of the month. Now throw on top of that the fact his returning players finished last in the PAC-10. I wondered if Barbara told him the whole story, because Jim was walking into a potential disaster.

Jim hired his brother, Rick, to be one of his assistants that first year. The athletic department had hired UW volleyball legend and Hall of Fame member Leslie Tuiasosopo to a one-year assistant-coach contract prior to Coach Neville's resignation. During the negotiation, Barbara Hedges told Jim the only preexisting condition was he had to keep Leslie for at least one year. As Jim related the story to me a few months later, he told Barbara, "I want to hire my own staff."

"You can hire an assistant and a graduate assistant, but we have a contract and a commitment to Leslie for this season."

Jim asked, "Is she related to Marques Tuiasosopo?" Marques is also a beloved UW legend and Hall of Fame football quarterback. He is the last quarterback to lead the Huskies to a Rose Bowl victory.

"Yes. She is his sister."

"So if this doesn't work out after one year and I let her go, I will be hated by everyone in Seattle."

Barbara replied, "Don't be silly. It won't just be the people of Seattle. The entire Northwest will hate you. So I suggest you make this work."

This has never been an issue. Nine years later, Leslie is associate head coach and the recruiting coordinator.

* * *

Sherry, the new team administrator, scheduled a POINT! HUSKIES! board meeting with Jim McLaughlin prior to the first preseason tournament. The meeting was short and to the point. Jim said, "I don't have and won't have much time to spend with this group this season. I have never had or wanted to meet with a booster group this large on a regular basis. I suggest you prepare a plan of what you want to do and what you need me to do, and we will discuss it in a few weeks. So all of you know, my plan is to win the national title within five years. I don't know what we have this year yet, but we will be better than last season.

The team will play with pride and passion. Everyone will see a major improvement in the level of play. Are there any questions before I have to leave?"

One board member asked, "How often are we going to meet with you to discuss events and plans?"

"We won't be meeting very often. I just won't have the time. Get your plan together and we'll talk in a few weeks. I am sorry to cut this short, but I have to review film from practice today." And with that he left.

The board members stuck around for several minutes discussing what just occurred. Two or three of the people were offended by the brevity and abruptness of the meeting. Comments ranged from, "That was rude," to "He can't be serious. There is no way this program can win a National Title in five years." I was very impressed with the guy. He was a no-nonsense leader who clearly stated his goals for the program and the level of involvement he wanted with a booster group. To me it sounded like this group was going to be more business and results oriented or it simply was not going to exist. As we left the meeting, I said to Sherry, "I am really impressed. I look forward to working with Jim."

Sherry replied, "Many of the people in this group are not going to like or want to work with Jim. He is not going to run the meetings, and he certainly isn't going to spend the time telling stories about the Olympics."

"That's good news," was my response. "The meetings last year were a waste. We never got around to doing anything of value."

As we walked out to the parking lot, Sherry said, "I will set up a one-on-one meeting between you and Jim when things start to settle down. You are one of the few people who want to see this organization run more like a business. Keep working on your plan, and I'll let you know when he has some time to meet."

The team did play with significantly more passion. Jim just had the returning players from last season and two freshmen that he had not recruited. My heart went out to the two freshmen. It had to be very difficult for them. One of the freshmen,

Kaitlin Leck, made a significant contribution during her four years. The other left the program after her first year.

The preseason practices were spent teaching a very new system, moving players into new roles and positions. The most significant move was Gretchen Maurer to setter. Gretchen played with great intensity. She got the most out of Allison Richardson and Paige Benjamin on the outside, and Lisa Underhill became a force in the middle. The team won five of its first seven matches. The fans were starting to come back, and everyone commented on the players' aggressive and focused level of play.

Sherry scheduled the meeting between Jim and me just before the start of the PAC-10 season. I told him the team looked much better. "They seem to be playing with a purpose."

"We have a long way to go. It's going to take some time and patience."

"Jim, after what we have been through, to see the team hustling and playing hard again has the fans feeling hopeful."

"Frank, I wanted to meet with you because you seem to understand. I have never had a big group of people making demands on my time. I've met with a few of the people, but it seems they are more interested in me leading this group. I don't have the time or the desire. From what I have seen, you appear to understand and have a more businesslike approach."

"I am glad to hear you say that, Jim, because if things were going to stay the way they were last year, I don't want any part of the booster group."

"It looks like we understand each other. Let me tell you about my plan." Jim handed me a two-page document which outlined his strategy, philosophy, and goals. "We are going to win the national title in five years."

"That's a huge leap, Jim."

"I didn't say we will do it with this group. But this university has the facilities and the resources to attract the talent we need."

I glanced down at the paper and asked, "What is this cauldron?"

"I am an engineer by education. I rely on facts and numbers, not hunches and gut feelings. I work with empirical data. The cauldron is how we measure and monitor progress. We film every practice. We record the results of every drill. Then we rank each player in each position. The cauldron results are posted every day so everyone knows where she stands and what she needs to improve upon. The players with the highest scores play."

"That is a great approach, Jim. One of the issues last year was 'he likes her better, that's why I'm not playing.' This cauldron takes away that issue."

"Exactly!" Jim stood up and became more animated as he explained "This allows me and the players to focus on volleyball. I also rely heavily on video. We film every practice and match. We review practice video everyday with the players, sometimes as a group and sometimes individually. The players actually see what they did and what I want them to do almost immediately. There are no small things in volleyball. We go over every detail. I can tell you with a high probability where the ball is going based on how they receive the serve and where the setter receives the pass. The players will be moving to defend the high-probability area before the setter releases the ball. I call this movement patterns. It is almost like a dance."

"Wow, this is amazing. I never realized all the complexities and details. What do you need from me?"

"Sherry told me you were writing a business plan for the program. I'd love to see it."

"That's right. The plan is done. The goal is to generate revenue with as little involvement of the players and coaches as possible. We need to be smart and target specific donors. We need to create a newsletter, which I will write, and have it sent out to each donor and fan monthly. We need to make a connection between this program and the community. We need a list of equipment you need so I can show it to potential donors. This way they can select a specific item or multiple items. We need to have a consistent story about why you need this equipment and what value it will bring to the team. Husky fans want to feel like they have a part or a role with the team. As long at the kids play hard every night, these fans will love you and support you forever. When you win the national title, you will achieve legend status. I am so excited. I'll tell you what, Jim, you coach your team and I will find a way to raise some money."

"Good. Now this is important. I only want to interface with you, Frank. I don't want to deal with ten or fifteen people. How do we do that?"

"That part is easy. We will finalize the plan, and then set a board meeting. You start the meeting, and then turn it over to me, and you leave. I will present the plan and see who buys in. My guess is most people won't participate. This will bring the group down to a few people who are actually interested in helping the program and executing the plan. I do turn-arounds of failing companies for a living. I go through this every day. We will find out which people are going to step up and which ones are going to stand on the sidelines and wait for us to fail."

"We aren't going to fail, Frank."

"I will have the final version ready after this weekend. Good luck against Cal and Stanford." As I turned to leave, Jim asked me, "Frank, what do you want out of this?" My answer was, "I want to hold the national championship trophy."

I drove home excited about where this program was about to go. The team beat Cal on Friday and pushed Stanford to four games before losing the fourth game, 33-31. The crowd was in a frenzy. I had never heard the arena so loud. Everyone was pleased and excited about how the team played. As I left the arena, I saw Jim and the assistant coaches walking out of their office. I called out to them, "Great game, coaches."

Jim said with frustration, "We had them on the ropes more than once and couldn't close the deal."

"Jim, you don't understand. The crowd loved the energy and the passion. Everyone can see the team is getting better. That's all anyone expects this year. Just get better and play with fire and passion. You won over a lot of new fans today."

Chapter 4

TURN-AROUND RULE #2—CLEARLY ARTICULATE THE VISION

* * *

If you don't know where you are going, you'll never know if you get there. Every organization must have a vision or a plan. Everyone must know that vision and make it his or her own.

Jim McLaughlin's vision was very simple.

1. Graduate every player.
2. Finish in the top three in the PAC-10 every year. This gives the team the opportunity to compete for the national title.
3. Prepare players for the U.S. national team.

Jim's plan was simple and concise. Executing it was the challenge. His first team ended the year 11-16 and in eighth place in the PAC-10. This was up two places from the previous year. The wheels were in motion. My challenge was to come up with a business plan to help raise the additional funds and fan support to make this vision a reality. We only generated about $7,000 that first season, but the team made progress, and I had something to work with.

Following is the initial business plan.

POINT! HUSKIES! Plan

Table of Contents
Mission Statement
Goal of POINT! HUSKIES!
Proposed Board Structure
Situation Analysis
Product: What Are We Selling?
People: Target Audience
Placement: Marketplace and Competition
Promotion: How Do We Sell What We're Selling?
S.W.O.T Analysis
Strengths:
Weaknesses:
Opportunities:
Threats:
Where Do We Want to Go?
Budget Summary
How Do We Get There?
Action Plan
POINT! HUSKIES Newsletter

POINT! HUSKIES!

Mission Statement

POINT! HUSKIES! is an organization dedicated to generating personal and financial support for the University of Washington Women's Volleyball program.

By increasing our annual membership donations and constantly improving our methods, we will be a proactive partner with Husky volleyball in its pursuit of PAC-10 and national championships.

POINT! HUSKIES! board members must be donors at the $500 level.

Goal of POINT! HUSKIES!

POINT! HUSKIES! is an organization dedicated to supporting the University of Washington's women's volleyball program. This support comes in many forms, such as planning events for the players and their parents; community outreach programs; and camps and clinics throughout the year. The main function of POINT! HUSKIES!! is fundraising.

Membership in POINT! HUSKIES!! is open to everyone with a passion for volleyball and the University of Washington. Our membership goals are threefold:

1. Fill our beautiful new Bank of America Arena with wildly enthusiastic fans.
2. Build generations of Husky volleyball supporters.
3. Raise the funds needed to make Husky volleyball the envy of every university.

Proposed Board Structure

1. President—two-year term. The president will oversee the activities of the various committees and be the primary interface to the team/program coordinator.
2. Fundraising Chair—three-year term. Will design and develop programs such that each program can generate a minimum of $5,000 in revenue (for example, cocktail parties, golf event, etc.).
3. Game Events—three-year term. Will design and develop programs that will generate involvement between the program and the community. Examples of game events include teams of greeters at games (say hello and thank you to everyone; give them game day material, calendars, etc; answer questions and say thank you and hope to see you at the next game; hand out newsletters/player profiles/question of the game; hand out and collect information cards from game attendees; news letter etc.; nominate honorary coach at home games. Grassroots fundraising events, such as selling raffle tickets, taking pictures during games for promotions and recruiting).
4. Community Outreach will be handled by the coaching staff. Ideas or suggestions for outreach programs are to be sent to Sherry. The coaching staff will make the final decisions regarding community outreach programs.

Newsletters mailed per schedule listed in this plan. It will be e-mailed to the sign-up list that we collect at every match to push information to interested people.

All proposed events and fundraising plans **must** come with a business plan that includes:

1. Description of event
2. Target audience
3. Cost
4. Estimated dates
5. Expected revenue to the volleyball program

6. Staffing
7. Probability of success

We do not have the donor or attendance base to support several fundraising events. Given this situation, we will limit the number of fundraising events to those that give us the best chance for success.

For calendar year 2001, POINT! HUSKIES! fundraising should limited to two activities:

1. Direct request for donations. Ten to twelve key individuals have been targeted. A donation plan is under development to raise the $50,000 goal.
2. The raffle for a new car. This is an athletic department function designed to support all Olympic sports.

The events volunteers have the challenge to increase attendance at our matches. As attendance grows, we will look at other fundraising events.

Situation Analysis

Product: What Are We Selling?
- A Washington-based Pac-10 Conference Women's Volleyball Program
- A head coach with a men's national championship and women's top-fifteen program
- The best volleyball conference in the world
- The opportunity to watch the development of a world-class player(s)

People: Target Audience
- Women (all ages)
- Local volleyball fans (men/women)
- UW students
- UW sports fans
- Alumni
- Inclusive families and employers

Placement: Marketplace and Competition
- Marketplace: private and corporate donations (without conflicting with marketing)
- Competition:
    - Youth/club programs
    - Strong fall sports programs (football, men's/women's soccer, crew)
    - Seattle professional sports team (football and basketball)

Promotion: How Do We Sell What We're Selling?
- The experience:
    - Game attendance
    - Promotions
    - Bank of America Arena
    - Player profiles and questions of day (like baseball)

- Fundraising:
  - Membership
  - Raffle
  - Continous solication of donations at events—letters, newsletter,

S.W.O.T Analysis

Strengths:

1. Level of competition (Pac-10 conference)
2. Proven coaching staff
3. Facilities—Bank of America Arena, training facilities, beauty of the campus

Weaknesses:

1. Nonqualifier for NCAA Tournament since 1997
2. Low PAC-10 finish
3. Losses to closest in-state and out-of-state rivals

Opportunities:

1. Rising interest and participation in women's volleyball (scholastic, club, etc.)
2. Coaches' clinics
3. Summer camp and off-season clinics at junior high and grade schools

Threats:

1. Strong UW fall sports programs (football, men's/women's soccer, crew, all national powers)
2. Strong youth programs (football, soccer)
3. Low-revenue sport—lack of media exposure
4. Professional sports(Sonics, Seahawks, Mariner's playoffs)

Where Do We Want to Go?

We are promoting the **experience** of and the **association** with Husky volleyball. We are competing for the entertainment dollars of our target audience. They must feel a connection with the program that is strong enough to makes them want to attend matches and/or support the program as sponsors and donors. Relationship development with the target market (**women**) is critical.

Any decision to buy requires a transfer of emotion. The buyer must feel both a relationship **and** a comfort level before a purchase can occur. Creating **a positive emotional attachment** with the products produces a sales opportunity.

To remain competitive in the Seattle sports entertainment market, Husky volleyball needs to **create and retain** customers. Our challenge is magnified by several subpar seasons. Many former fans have found other sources for their entertainment dollar. Engaging the target audience in communication about the **new era** of Washington volleyball starts this process. Maintaining the connection by pushing interesting information about the program will build awareness and presents the opportunity for the relationship to develop. **Repeated contact** gradually builds customer confidence which leads to the buying decision.

Game-day promotions and advertising will be created to maximize the "experience" and "association." Game day is "show time"— customers now become **guests**. How the guest is treated before and after the match is as important as the quality of the match. Guests must receive a warm greeting as they enter the arena and be offered game-day material by a POINT! HUSKIES! member. Each guest should be directed to pick up or be handed a POINT! HUSKIES! information card (name, address, e-mail, would they like to receive the newsletters, favorite Husky player, tell me more about POINT! HUSKIES! etc.) and team giveaway (calendar, poster etc.). An announcement at the match promoting POINT! HUSKIES! should occur. At the end of the match, guests should also receive a personal "thank you for coming and we hope to see you at our next match" message from a POINT!

HUSKIES! member. POINT! HUSKIES! members should wear the same volleyball apparel with a sign or button saying, "Ask me about POINT! HUSKIES!" Youth teams in uniforms at the games should be on court for the national anthem—this is a great time to find ball people for the matches and make a connection with 'junior volleyball' players; honorary coach introduction should be before player introduction, and they should go on court with the starters.

A quarterly newsletter during the off-season and monthly in season will keep the current and potential boosters informed. This must be part of a yearlong membership plan driven by the membership chair. Included will be an event day booth or table to promote POINT! HUSKIES! membership. In addition, POINT! HUSKIES! president and/or membership chair will make monthly visits to targeted donors.

Special events will include a spring tournament/meet the players, alumni game/kickoff banquet, a possible golf tournament, and the annual raffle. Apparel sales will be promoted on a yearlong basis to offer the opportunity to **"wear what the team wears."**

Community outreach programs such as skills clinics conducted by the players at Seattle area schools (elementary, junior highs, club teams, YMCA, etc.) and coaches' clinics serve two purposes. First, they introduce the "experience" and "association." Second, they reinforce the positive emotional attachment. Information about summer camps will be given out and newsletters will also be used to maintain contact.

The resulting goal is to increase membership and revenue to make Husky volleyball the envy of every university. Creative and proactive relationship management is the foundation to build strong program support. Under Coach McLaughlin's direction, it is only a matter of time before our Huskies become a fixture in the "Sweet 16" and "Final Four." Let's make sure we have provided the necessary financial and emotional support.

Chapter 5

TURN-AROUND RULE #3—INSPIRE PEOPLE TO BELIEVE

* * *

The 2001 season started a "buzz" around the program. Returning players were excited again. They saw the improvement the first year and knew the program was attracting better athletes to consider UW. Jim's first camps sold out quickly, and he started the process of selling UW to the next generation of Washington-based players.

After the first season, Jim's brother left the coaching staff. The plan was for him to stay just one year to help Jim get ready quickly. Pat Stangle joined Leslie Tuiasosopo as assistant coach. The coaches met with and held coaching clinics for nearly every club program in the state. The idea was to teach the UW way of playing volleyball to build the experience and association with the program. If done correctly, UW would be the first choice for every volleyball player in the state. Once we secured the state of Washington, the program could expand to other areas. The challenge in 2001 and early 2002 was the lack of PAC-10 level volleyball players living in Washington. The outreach was more to start the development of younger players and start to build a pipeline for the future.

We scheduled some lunches and golf for Jim with some prominent donors. This allowed people with means to start an association with a program that was on the rise. The great thing about the people of Seattle is as long as you give your best effort and represent UW with character and class; your program will be supported. If you become an elite program that either wins or annually contends for the PAC-10 and national titles, you will be revered.

We scheduled a cocktail party for hand-selected donors at Barbara Hedges home. Many of these donors were new to volleyball and didn't understand many of the rules or the strategy of the game. The plan was for Jim to bring video so he could explain what the team was trying to do at a particular point in a game and then show the video. When he has video, Jim becomes on par with President Obama as an orator. He is so comfortable breaking down film. He would stop the video and point out what was about to occur and why. For example, "the other team's middle blocker was disrupting our offense." He explained what was going to occur to freeze this blocker and open up an alley for the UW hitter. He would then run the video, and you could hear "oohhs and ahhs" throughout the room. Most people said they had no idea there was so much strategy involved. They were in awe, and we left with over $5,000 in donations.

The community was becoming inspired. Now the challenge was to get the right players into the program.

Chapter 6

TURN-AROUND RULE #4—CLEARLY DEFINE WHAT THE LEADER WANTS AND WHAT PIECES ARE NEEDED

* * *

As exciting as 2001 was, the program needed a strong recruiting year. A large freshmen class was coming in. Seven freshmen entered the program. It is unheard of to have seven freshmen in one season. It is equally unheard of that six players stay the full four years. This freshmen class redefined UW volleyball. It included Sanja Tomesevic and Danka Danicic both from Serbia, Darla Myhre, Candace Lee, Jessica Veris, and Carolyn Farney. This was Jim's first recruiting class, and several were going to have to contribute immediately.

Gretchen Maurer and Paige Benjamin were battle tested as setter and outside hitter and undersized but overachieving Kara Bjorklund (KB) had worked her way into the middle blocker role, but they weren't enough. The first player to commit to UW was Candace Lee. She had been an outside hitter in high school but lacked the size to play the position in the PAC-10. What Candace could do, however, was keep the ball from hitting the ground (dig), which prevented the opponent from scoring. She could also pass the ball to the exact spot where the setter needed it to run the offense. She was recruited to play the new defensive specialist position called the libero. Two returning players believed they had the inside track for this position. But as they found out, seniority is not part of the UW system. The player that scores the best in practice plays. Candace was very, very good. The libero wore a different color jersey and could only play in the back row. This new position was confusing to Husky fans, so we prepared a game-day handout which explained the position. Candace was so good that she became a crowd favorite. It was not usual to see signs in the arena that read "Candace would have dug that" when our opponent could not dig a ball. I am not saying Candace invented the position, but if you look up the definition of "libero," her picture should be there. Candace would anchor the back row.

Danka Danicic came to Washington from Serbia. She was a defensive specialist whose role was to complement Candace. She would also replace one of the middle hitters when they rotated to the back row. This gives the team a better passer and defender. If a team can't pass well, a team can't win. Finally, she had to be able to come in off the bench and make critical serves. No pressure there!

Now Jim needed people who could attack and score points. The answer came from Serbia. Sanja Tomasevic, a twenty-two-year-old, internationally tested player, enrolled at UW. She had been unable to start college due to the civil war in Serbia. Sanja was a member of the Serbian national team and played in several major international tournaments. How Sanja ended up in Washington is an amazing story. She and I had a long conversation recently. Her story is intriguing.

* * *

Sanja's college career was delayed by the civil war in Serbia. At age twenty-two, she was at a crossroads. She had three options:

1.   Stay with the Serbian national team.
2.   Turn professional.
3.   Come to the United States for college.

She and her family were leaning heavily toward option three. Once her resume, film, and background became available, offers started to roll in. Sanja told me, "I didn't know much about American volleyball at the time. I certainly didn't know the PAC-10 from the SEC from Division Three schools. One of the first schools to contact me was St. Louis Baptist. I had no idea about their level of volleyball. I was also hoping to go to a school that had a Serbian player. At that time only the University of South Carolina had one. It was suggested that I expand my profile. So I added my preference to attend a school in a warm-weather state close to the beach" she said, laughing. "After all everyone wants to hang out at the beach."

"I was told given my experience I should limit my search to the PAC-10. The three recommended schools were UCLA, USC, and Washington. I went online and discovered that all three were close to the Pacific Ocean, so that met my beach requirement. Although I didn't realize going to beach in Seattle is much different than in LA." She laughed again. "I made contact with each program. They all sounded good. USC and UCLA said I would be starting immediately. Jim said with his program everyone has to earn playing time. I recall telling him, 'I'm not coming to America to sit on the bench!' He told me, 'If you work hard and follow our program, you will play. But we don't make guarantees.'"

"As I continued my research, I discovered that UCLA and USC had won the national championship multiple times. Washington had never been to a Final Four. I was so confused." Then she said, laughing, "I even started to look at the school colors to see which one I would look best in."

"I talked to my father and told him that USC and UCLA said I would start immediately but Washington would not make a guarantee. My father's response was, 'I raised you better than that. What do you want to do, take the easy way out? How can these coaches promise you anything, they don't even know you! All they have is a short video. The coach at Washington is the only one being honest with you. Nobody gives you anything in life. You have to earn whatever you get. You know that.' At first I was very upset, but as I thought about what he said, I knew he was right."

"I finally found an e-mail address for Vesna Dragicevic, a former member of the Serbian national team who played volleyball at USC. I wrote to her and asked if she would help me with my decision. She told me she would be happy to help me, and she was pleased that I was willing to make this step. She wrote, 'When I left, I was pressured by the national team. They told me if I left, I could never come back. I was so upset that after all the years I played on the national team, they would ban me because I was doing something that would improve my life. Maybe if you leave, it will encourage other Serbian girls to follow their dreams.' I told her I had narrowed my choices to USC, UCLA, and Washington. She asked me, 'What are you looking for in a school?' I wrote back, 'I want a good academic school and I want to play for a coach who will make me better because I want to play professionally after college.' Her response was interesting. She said, 'Each school has excellent academics, but the best coach, the one that will make you the best player you can be, is Jim McLaughlin at Washington. He was the men's coach at USC when I played. I saw what he did with the men's team. He also would help out with the women's team. If your plan is to play professionally after college or develop into an Olympic level player, then play for Jim McLaughlin.'

"I contacted Jim and we started the process. I also received a phone call from Danka Danicic's father. I didn't know Danka well, but I knew she played for another team in Serbia. Her father said, 'Danka is considering Washington, and we heard you are planning to go to Washington. Can we drive over to your home and talk to you and your family?' Danka and her family drove over two hours and we all talked. I said to Danka, 'If we go to USC or UCLA, we will be one of two or three hundred players who won the national championship. If we go to Washington, we will be the first players to win.' We agreed we wanted to make history. The decision was made. Danka and I would go to Washington. On June 3, my birthday, I signed my letter of intent. We then scheduled a time visit UW."

I said to Sanja, "I heard the trip turned into an adventure." She laughed and said, "You aren't going to believe this. I was booked from Serbia through London to Seattle. When I arrived in London, I was told I needed something called a transit visa. I never heard of this, so I was sent back home. I called Jim and told him want happened. We rescheduled the trip, and I went to the British Embassy to obtain a transit visa. The day I arrived at the embassy, the entire area had a power failure and they could not print the transit visa. So I had to wait another couple of days. Then, finally, I arrive in Seattle, and the airline loses my luggage."

I said to Sanja, "After all this aggravation, I am amazed you still came to Washington." Sanja's response was, "There is an old Serbian saying that goes something like this: 'the more difficulty or the more obstacles you have to overcome to achieve your goal or dream, the greater your reward will be at the end.' My father told me, 'After all you went through to go to UW, you should live in the White House.' After we won the national championship, I called my father from the White House and told him I just met the president of the United States. It was the first time I ever heard my father's voice crack with emotion. He was so proud. Who would have ever imagined that a girl from a war-torn country who had to wait until twenty-two to start college would be a national champion, All-American, player of the year, and meet the president of the United States?"

That story brought tears to my eyes.

* * *

Sanja was and arguably still is the best volleyball player to ever attend UW. She became the cornerstone of this program. Sanja was older than the other players, was more mature, and had more experience competing at the highest level. She was the "real deal." She could play the left or right side. She could block at the net. She could launch an attack starting behind the 10-foot line. She could pass from the back row almost as well as Candace, and she had a "wicked" jump serve. Sanja and setter Gretchen Maurer were named captains. With Sanja in the fold, UW secure commitments from Darla Myhre, a six-foot-two-inch middle blocker from British Columbia, Jessica Veris, a highly coveted player from Southern California, Carolyn Farney, and Danka.

The pieces were in place for UW to secure its first NCAA bid since 1997. The team started the pre-PAC-10 season 10-1, with the only loss coming on the road against national power Hawaii.

The fans and student body were geared up for the PAC-10 season, and the team did not disappoint. The level of play was greatly improved. The freshmen played with unbridled energy. Husky fans had not seen this type of power, speed, and finesse. Crowds increased to 1,500 to 1,700 per match. This was unheard of in the past.

We tried to limit the number of events during the season. We did schedule a white-board conversation with Jim McLaughlin before the UCLA match. We invited donors and a number of volleyball alumni to come back for this match and attend the event. Leslie handled the contact with the former players. Most of the alumni who committed to attend had played with Leslie, so she would be the focal point for the event. This was the first time we tried a game day event. Jim was not comfortable changing his game day routine but agreed to come in, say hello, and talk about the strategy for UCLA. We had a fairly good turnout over one hundred people. The alumni seemed to enjoy seeing each other again. None of them had met Jim and were very interested in seeing and hearing what he had to say. Leslie came up with the white board that Jim had just reviewed with the team. The board was covered with notes, drawing, quotes etc.; Jim loves using two things when he coaches or talks. Video is his first love, and a white board is a close second.

Jim looked very uncomfortable when he entered the room. I quickly got everyone's attention and said, "We only have Coach McLaughlin for a few minutes. Coach, UCLA has been a challenge for us in the past. What can we expect to see tonight?"

Jim went right into coach mode. "The key tonight is to hold their middle blocker so she can't help out with the outside block. This means Candace, our libero, the one wearing a different-colored jersey, will have to be near perfect with her passes to Gretchen, our setter. Watch Gretchen tonight. If she had to move her feet to get the pass from Candace, we could have some problems. If Gretchen gets the pass where she is standing, then she will set our middles, Darla and KB. We have to establish that we can score from our middles early. Once we have established the middle, look for Gretchen to go to Paige and Sanja on the outside. This will give Paige and Sanja one blocker to beat. If we execute this strategy, we will win." Jim then left the event to go back with the team, who was warming up.

UCLA was loaded. They had swept us 3-0 several weeks earlier in Los Angeles. In fact we hadn't beaten UCLA anywhere since 1997. The match started, and everything Jim had on the board was happening. Candace and Danka were passing the ball to spot where Gretchen was standing. Gretchen was able to make the quick, short set to Darla and KB for the point. UW won the first game 30-28 and the second 30-27. As the match progressed, you could see the UCLA middle blocker freeze an extra split second to make sure the ball didn't go to our middle hitters in the third game. This opened up the outsides and UW won the third game 30-22. Not only did the team beat UCLA, they swept UCLA. The big crowd was going crazy. No one left the arena for a good ten to fifteen minutes. The noise level was amazing. Everyone could sense the wave of change was occurring.

The team ended the season 20-11 and 9-9 in the PAC-10. UW was not only selected to the NCAA Tournament, but they made it to the second round before losing to nemesis Hawaii. Paige Benjamin was named First Team All American. This was the first Husky All American since Laurie Wetzel in 1998. Gretchen Maurer and Sanja were named to the All-PAC-10 team. Fundraising increased to over $20,000, and one family purchased $11,000 worth of video equipment. The ball was rolling.

Chapter 7

TURN-AROUND RULE #5—SELECT THE RIGHT PEOPLE AND PUT THEM IN THE BEST POSITION TO SUCCEED

* * *

The most difficult task in turning around any organization is evaluating and or replacing the people you inherit. These people were there before the new leader and obviously have some vested interest in the organization's success. No one wants to fail, but the reason the new leader enters the picture is because things aren't working.

Whenever I started a new turn-around job, I gave everyone the benefit of the doubt up front. I would meet with the entire staff together and outline the vision. I would say there are things that are going to change. We will keep what is working and change or discard what isn't working. Then I would give everyone the book *Who Moved My Cheese,* by Spencer Johnson. I would give everyone time to read it on company time.

The next step was to meet with each one individually to gauge if he or she was receptive to the message. Of course, everyone tells you at the first one-on-one that he or she is on board. I got a pretty good idea from people's reactions to the book. The ones who saw themselves as one of the mice were open to trying new and hopefully better ways. The ones who said they didn't understand why I gave them a book about mice were more than likely not going to make it.

The next step was to observe and monitor progress. Talk is cheap. Many inherited people will not engage. Many prefer to stay on the sidelines and make their own decision as to just how committed the new leader is to his or her vision. Hopefully, most of the inherited people buy into the program and are willing to change. Those that change can be valuable assets. Those who refuse have to be let go so the leader can bring in new people.

I read the book *From Good to Great,* by Jim Collins. I gave a copy to Jim McLaughlin and set a time to meet to discuss some of the concepts. The two things from the book that jumped out to both of us were:

1. Get the right people on the bus and the wrong people off the bus.
2. The hedgehog theory (this will be discussed in a later chapter).

Every leader will tell you, his or her most valuable asset is the employees. That is not really the case. What we discovered in this book is that the most valuable asset is *the right people.* The right people understand and accept the vision. The right people are motivated and driven. The right people are both ready and able to execute. The wrong people do none of these things. The wrong people lower standards. The wrong people drive away the right people.

I have had the following conversation with many leaders. Here is the scenario. "You have nine people. Three are outstanding, three are average to mediocre, and three are substandard. What do you do?" My first response, like most people, is to leave the three outstanding people alone. I get rid of the substandard people, and I spend my time trying to raise the level of the average people. What I derived from the book is that this course of action is a recipe for failure. As a leader, I should focus on the outstanding people and get rid of the average and substandard. I should be constantly looking to add the right people to my organization. I have heard many leaders say, "My job is to motivate people." Again, Mr. Collins points out, this is wrong. The leader's job is not to motivate; it is to not demotivate the right people. The right people are already motivated. When the right people see the leader focused on the average people, it sends a message that he or she is willing to accept mediocrity. It says. "I am not willing to surround you with more of the right people." This tends to demotivate the right people, who either lower their level or, the more likely scenario, they leave the organization.

In college athletics, this means recruiting the right people for your program. This does not mean if you get all the most physically gifted athletes, then success is guaranteed. Rather, this means you get the right people to fit into your program. I read an article many years ago in the *Harvard Business Review* about Red Auerbach (the legendary champion coach of the Boston Celtics) and his view on management. The main point was, he had a system. He needed people at each job who were willing to accept their role (job description). He selected people who understood that the collective contribution of like-minded people would produce a result greater than what could be achieved alone. He often passed on a more talented person if that person was more interested in his or her individual success rather than that of the organization.

* * *

The 2002 season was full of change and drama. With seven incoming freshmen, everything was going to change. The freshman had to learn everything, from how to be a college student to finding their way around campus to enrolling in classes to the total and complete overhaul of their volleyball game. "I thought I knew how to play this game," said Sanja, "but once practice started, Jim changed everything about my game and everyone else's, too. At first we were all a little reluctant to change. After one particularly frustrating practice, Jim told me, 'Sanja do you want a coach who is going to let you stay the way you are? Or do you want to become the best player you can be?' I said, 'I want to be the best, but it doesn't seem I can do anything right! I know how to play this game. That's why you brought me here.' I will never forget his answer. He said, 'You are here because you are good. You have all the necessary tools to become great. The question to you is this: are you willing to become great? Moving from good to great is not easy. It requires you to examine and reexamine every aspect of your game and your life. It requires your total and complete commitment. If you are willing to learn and have the *courage* to change your game, your attitude, your diet, your training, and your behavior outside of this court, you could become great.'

"I wasn't sure how to react. At first I thought the man was crazy. He told us before the first practice that we are going to win the national title within four years. This program with seven freshmen was going to win the national title before I graduate. After that first practice, I said to myself, 'He has to be crazy. There is no way this group is going to win the league, let alone the national title, and now he wants me to reinvent myself.' To make matters worse, Carl McGowan, one of Jim's mentors, was at one of the early practices, and I heard him say, 'Jim, you missed with Sanja. She isn't quick enough, she doesn't jump high enough, and she is going to fight you every step along the way.' I was so hurt and angry when I heard that, but I didn't run away and cry. I went to Jim and asked, 'Is that what you think of me?' Jim told me, 'I believe you could become the PAC-10 and national player of the year. But this is not just about you. You have to become the leader of this program. We have six other freshmen who look to you for everything. Plus, potential recruits will come here based on how well you progress. You can be just another good player, or you could become the first piece of a great program'. I left Jim's office determined to show Carl he was wrong."

✳ ✳ ✳

As Jim McLaughlin began the 2002 season, most of the inherited players saw the improvement and bought into the program. There were three who did not. As I heard the story from several sources, they felt entitled to a starting position based on their seniority at the school. They brought a less-than-enthusiastic attitude to practice. The freshmen were excited and eager to perform, but their enthusiasm and passion were constantly stifled. A series of heated conversations occurred between the players. Some of the freshmen left practice in tears, feeling they made a terrible mistake coming to UW. Jim met with some of the freshmen and asked, 'What's wrong?' He knew he had a problem with the three players but wanted to hear from the freshmen if there was another issue that had them so upset. When each refused to give Jim the real reason, he knew things had gone far enough, and the three players were dismissed from the team. A players-only meeting occurred the same night. The remaining players were able to air issues and grievances. The younger players expressed that they wanted to play with passion and show that passion when a good play occurred. Some of the older players didn't believe the show of passion was appropriate. The three international freshmen all pointed out that most national teams, including the U.S. team whom they had all played against, all showed passion after a key play. The freshmen stated they were not comfortable or relaxed and consequently not enjoying the experience. To the credit of the captains, Gretchen Maurer and freshman Sanja, the team agreed to relax and play with passion even if it meant faking it. As Sanja said to me, "The first couple of practices after the meeting had a few exaggerated displays of emotion, but all-of-a-sudden all the players started to cheer and compliment an outstanding play or effort. We started encouraging and cheering for each other. We started to hold each other accountable when we knew someone didn't make a good effort. We started to come together as a team and a program."

At the end of the 2002 season, Jim had his mentor, Carl McGowan, perform a detailed assessment of the strengths, weaknesses, and needs of the program. Jim and Carl had been part of USA Volleyball together. Carl was a PhD from Oregon in motor learning, the psychology of movement. He had taught at the University of California at Berkeley (Cal) and Brigham Young University (BYU). Carl discovered his true passion in life was working with volleyball players, coaches, and programs.

I asked Jim about Carl before the assessment. "I met Carl at USA Volleyball many years ago. We were assistants on the national team for Marv Dunphy. We were getting ready to play Brazil, who was just killing everyone. Marv had asked all the staff to prepare an assessment and strategy on how to beat Brazil. All the assistants got up one at a time and offered their opinions, ideas, and their 'gut feelings' on how to play Brazil. I did the same as the others. But Carl was different; he had film and a white board already prepared. He said, 'Our opinions, ideas, and feelings don't mean a damn thing. This is what they are doing on offense. Here are their patterns and tendencies based on where the pass is coming from. This is what we have to stop.' He did the same thing with their defense patterns and tendencies. That day was the single greatest training I ever received as a coach. Coaches can say this is what they want to do or this is our philosophy, but it doesn't mean that is what the other team is doing. The film doesn't lie. If you watch enough film and know how to break down film, you can set your plan of attack. Now if you have the players who can execute, you give yourself a chance to win."

"So Carl comes here, reviews your plans and strategies, and then compares them to what is on the film."

"That's right. The film doesn't lie. Plus, we look at every player. We match up what we are teaching them with what they are actually doing. This allows us to concentrate on specific areas of strength and weakness. The best teaching method is for the player to actually see what they are doing right and wrong."

* * *

The plan for 2003 was to fill the huge void left at setter and outside hitter from Gretchen's and Paige's graduations. Outside hitter Brie Hagerty transferred from Ohio State. Brie was a powerful hitter. She broke fingers, noses, and blackened eyes with her power. What she lacked in touch, she made up for with raw power. Jessica Veris and Kaitlin Leck were also more than capable on the outside.

The offense runs best when there are two strong middle blockers. Darla Myhre showed as a freshman that she would be one of the best in the league. Kara Bjorklund, an undersized senior from Tacoma, Washington, had staked her claim as the other middle blocker. "KB" showed Husky fans that heart and desire could make up for a lack of size. She was an inspiration to her teammates and fans.

Candace and Danka were solid in the back row, and Sanja was ready to become the next UW All American.

Despite all its offensive fire power, nothing happens unless you have a setter who can run the offense. The best player in the state of Washington was five-foot-eight setter Courtney Thompson. Courtney came from Kentlake High School, where she led her team to two consecutive state titles in 2000 and 2001. No one worked harder than Courtney. She worked so hard that she was in danger of hurting herself. A number of schools passed on Courtney. "Too short, too slow getting to the ball, bad hands, and a liability at the net" were the most common complaints. But Jim McLaughlin saw something the other coaches didn't. He didn't look at her height, he looked at her heart. He looked at her desire and drive to be the best. He looked at her will to win and to not let anyone on her team give less than her best.

Now UW had two of the key pieces in place. Sanja was the cornerstone of the program and Courtney became the heart and soul. Sanja and Courtney (just a freshman) were named captains. More of the right people were on the bus.

"The pieces are almost there for us to make a run at the PAC-10 title," Jim said, looking at the PAC-10 team statistics. "When I look at all the key measurable statistics, we are not quite there. Our attacks, the number of assists and blocks, are comparable to the top three teams in the PAC-10. But our service errors, serve receive errors, side out, and blocking has to get better."

The home crowds were starting to get larger and more vocal. The crowds were averaging over two thousand people. The students set up a section of the bleachers named the Dawg Pack, and they were loud. Donations keep increasing.

Chapter 8

TURN-AROUND RULE #6—FOCUS ON THE DETAILS AND TRAINING

* * *

Once the leader starts getting the right people on the bus, the leader has to make sure everyone knows not only what to do but how and why to do it. This comes from having a simple and consistent vision, processes, and procedures. Many leaders call this falling into a routine; I prefer to call it finding your stride. Consistency is now the key. Constant repetition or practice must occur. The leader at times seems like a broken record. Some people call this having a mantra. The leader must constantly preach three things:

1. This is what we do.
2. This is how we do it.
3. This is why we do what we do.

The 2002 season saw a quantum leap in the UW volleyball program: the first twenty-win season and NCAA tournament appearance since 1997. It was also the first win in the tournament since 1997. Hopes and expectations were high but guarded for 2003. The goal was to improve from fifth place in the PAC-10 to third place. The 2002 freshmen were a year older. Junior Kaitlin Leck and senior Kara Bjorklund (KB) were solid, stable performers. The big question mark was how well Courtney Thompson, a freshman setter, would run this team.

This team started off hot. It won the first eleven matches, including eight 3-0 sweeps. Wins number ten and eleven came against PAC-10 powers Arizona State and Arizona in Seattle. Next was the tortuous section of the PAC-10 season—four consecutive matches against the California schools, with consecutive matches against highly ranked Cal and Stanford on the road followed by even higher ranked USC (the defending national champions) and UCLA back in Seattle. The Huskies won the first game against Cal, and then lost the next three. Stanford swept the Huskies the next night. The team showed great heart against UCLA. After losing the first two games, they came back to tie the match at 2-2 before losing a heartbreaking fifth game 22-24 (remember the fifth game goes to 15). The defending champions from USC made short work of UW with a 3-0 sweep. The team found itself just 2-4 in the PAC-10.

Neither Jim McLaughlin nor the team panicked or become frustrated. They continued to work every day to get better. They focused on what they needed to do against their own standards and didn't worry about what higher-ranked PAC-10 teams did. "We can only control what we do," Jim repeated over and over. The team won the next three matches, and then it was back to the tortuous four matches against the California schools. This time the Huskies swept Stanford in Seattle. This was the first win against Stanford since 1993. The crowd went wild. Last year the long losing streak to UCLA ended and now Stanford. The celebration was short lived, since UW lost the next three matches to Cal, USC, and UCLA. The team once again regrouped and won five of its last six matches and a second consecutive NCAA tournament invitation.

This time around, UW easily won the first two matches in the tournament. They were back to the Sweet 16 for the first time since 1997. The fans were thrilled as the team headed to Long Beach to meet Stanford for the third time. Stanford was not pleased that its ten-year, twenty-consecutive-win streak against UW had ended. They were prepared to start another long winning streak. With one week to prepare for Stanford, the team focused on the film of the two Stanford matches. Since film doesn't lie, the coaches put together their plan of attack. The teams split the first two games. At the break, Jim McLaughlin fine-tuned the plan, which worked to perfection as the Huskies won the next two games. Stanford had been defeated twice in one year. The euphoria carried over to the Elite 8 match against Minnesota. The winner earned a berth to the Final Four. The teams split the first four games, so the Final Four would be determined by the fifth game tiebreaker. UW jumped out to a quick lead, but Minnesota would not be denied and ran off the last several points to win 15-9.

This loss left a very bitter taste in mouths of the players. "Six points, six lousy points, kept us from the Final Four," said a teary Sanja. The team was both angry and frustrated. The fans were elated. This program that most had written off for dead in 2000 had come within six points of the Final Four. None of us expected these kinds of results this soon. The fans showed their appreciation by breaking the $25,000 level in donations.

The 2003 team ended the season 23-9 and tied for fifth place in the PAC-10 for the second consecutive year. More important than the fifth-place finish was that the team now knew they could beat every PAC-10 team. They also knew what it took to get within six points of the Final Four. Focusing on the details and training, plus making sure everyone knew not only what to do but how and why to do it, brought this program its greatest success in the NCAA tournament. "Coming so close and not getting to the Final Four doesn't sit well with us" said Sanja. "No one went home that summer. Every returning player stayed and trained in Seattle. 'Six points' became our rally cry."

Sanja was named All American and All PAC-10. Also named to the All PAC-10 team were Kara Bjorklund, Darla Myhre, Candace Lee, and Courtney Thompson. This was the first time five Huskies were named to the All PAC-10 team.

Chapter 9

TURN-AROUND RULE #7—EVERYTHING IS DOCUMENTED; THE ORGANIZATION MUST OPERATE WITHOUT KEY PEOPLE PRESENT

* * *

Far too many organizations rely on word of mouth or the company grapevine to establish processes and procedures. This works if your organization is small with little to no turnover and people interact with each other daily. Most families use the word-of-mouth method. For example, curfew is midnight, or we work in the yard on Saturday mornings, etc. The family unit is usually small. The members see each other on a regular basis and, in general, the family unit stays together for several years.

In my first turn-around job, the company did not have any written policies, processes, or procedures. Everyone just knew what to do. So I asked, "How do they know?" I was told, "We don't have many people, so the most knowledge person in a particular area tells everyone else the process. Then it becomes a de-facto policy."

I then asked the question, "What happens when you bring in new people?" The answer was "We tell them what we do and they just figure it out by watching. If they get confused, they just ask and someone shows the new person what to do."

This led to my next question: "What if the person who knows the answer isn't there?" Answer, "In that case the person does the best they can or they get with another employee and they figure it out. Anyway, the person who established the policy is usually back the next day. So it's not a big deal."

Then I asked, "Wouldn't it make sense to write things down? At worst case the staff could use it as an instruction manual. Plus, it would avoid some of the freelancing that goes on here."

I was told, "Frank, we all worked for big companies or were in the military, and we all hated the bureaucracy. No one could do anything unless there was a policy or regulation or manual to read. We want a flat organization. We want people to be able to make a decision. Bureaucracy breeds complacency."

"So" I asked, "do you review these de-facto policies on a regular basis?"

"No, not usually. If something goes wrong, we talk about it and then decide what to change or do different the next time. We use the 'if it ain't broke, don't fix it' philosophy."

The next question was, "So how do you know if your processes are working or efficient or even cost effective?"

"Well, we just know. It takes too much time to sit down and write everything down. Once it is written down, then something changes, so we would never get anything done," was the answer.

Finally, in exasperation, I asked "Do you want this organization to grow and generate more revenue and profit?"

"Of course that's why we hired you."

"Then let me do what you are paying me to do."

I started out interviewing every department. I asked them to tell me exactly what they do. For example, "We receive purchase orders." Then I had them walk me through the entire process from the time the purchase order arrived until they received payment. It did not take long to create a work flow analysis and a written policy/procedure manual for each functional area. Whenever a new situation came up, the unit manager would simply document what occurred and what action they took to address the issue. Initially I would hold a short change management meeting weekly. We would go over the situation and try to determine if this was or could become a common occurrence. If the answer was yes, then we changed or updated the process. If the answer was no, then we would document the situation as an ad-hoc solution. If our policy/procedure manual covered 75 to 80 percent of the situations, I was happy.

The company did grow. We tripled in revenue and profit. We opened new offices and brought in new people. Since our policy/procedure manual covered 75 to 80 percent of situations, the organization was more efficient and profitable. This was not rocket science. It was simply creating a plan. As the late John Wooden said, "Failure to plan is planning to fail."

∗ ∗ ∗

Jim McLaughlin is a master at documentation. He thinks everything through with his staff and advisors. They create written practice plans, game plans, training plans, travel plans, meal plans, position plans, recruiting plans, official and unofficial visit plans, home visit plans, etc. Every day the white board was filled with the specific plan for that day.

In addition to the written plans Jim is a master with video. Every practice and every drill is recorded. A record of every drill is documented so both he and the players know how they did every day. All this data then went into the cauldron to calculate each player's ranking by position. The players with the highest scores by position played. Sanja told me, "You have no idea how wonderful the cauldron is for the players. We know exactly where we stand. We know who is going to play. If a player is not happy about her playing time, she knows what she needs to improve in practice. Jim always said, 'You can't have a lousy week of practice and play great on the weekend.'"

The staff had always "broken down" film on opponents. Again, every rotation, every serve, every set, every attack, and every point was documented and analyzed. Patterns and tendencies per team per situation were prepared. Jim told me, "I will always remember what Carl did at the USA Volleyball coaches' meeting. Film doesn't lie. Every team and coach develops tendencies. Once we know these tendencies, we know what we have to defend against and where they are most vulnerable to attack. Teams will follow their tendencies. So once we have a plan in place, we simply make in-match adjustments."

After the 2003 season, Jim had compiled three seasons' worth of film against the other PAC-10 schools and major NCAA tournament programs. The more data you have, the clearer the tendencies become and the easier it is to plan and make adjustments. I have never seen anyone better than Jim McLaughlin at in-game adjustments.

* * *

"'Six points.' Those two words haunted me," said Courtney Thompson. "I taped 'six points' in the weight room, on the team room door, on the mirrors, in my locker, on my car dashboard, and in my apartment. I couldn't look anywhere and not see 'six points.' I was obsessed with making it to the Final Four in 2004."

Three more of the right people came to the program for the 2004 season. The first was the highly recruited Christal Morrison. Christal was the Washington state player of the year and the number one recruit for several major programs. Christal had it all; height, reach, jumping ability, a strong arm, good blocking ability, and a great volleyball IQ. She made it look easy, almost effortless. "We didn't think Christal was going to UW," said her mother, Dianne Morrison. After living eighteen years in Western Washington, Christal had made it known she wanted to go someplace warm. She had ruled out USC and UCLA, but Arizona appeared to have the inside track. Dianne Morrison told me, "We agreed not to commit during the official visit to Arizona. We would see and hear what they had to say, then meet with UW and make a decision. Secretly, her dad and I hoped it would be UW so she would be close to home, but it was going to be her decision."

Christal once told me, "I played against Courtney in club and high school. Back then I didn't like her. I thought she was cocky and arrogant. There was no questioning that she was a winner. Maybe that is why I disliked her. But I saw her play and start as a freshman and nearly make the Final Four. I watched Sanja, who was tremendous, and something told me Sanja and I would be great together. Sanja was so good that teams had to focus on her. This would give me the opportunity to step in as a freshman without all the pressure of being the 'go-to' outside hitter."

Dianne Morrison said, "We took Chris to meet with Jim. It was a very cold and wet Seattle day. Since she had just returned from warm and sunny Arizona, I thought there was no way she would pick UW. We had a great meeting. Jim said the team would win the national title while Chris was at UW. I expected him to say that. I had talked with Linda Thompson, Courtney's mom, and she told me Jim told her the same thing. Linda said, 'When he told me that, I asked him if he had actually seen his team play, and if he thought he was going to do this with my little daughter that every school says is too small and too slow. Then in her freshman year they nearly make the Final Four. I stopped questioning Jim after that.' As we drove home, Chris was sitting in the back seat looking out at the rain; she suddenly sat up and announced, 'I am going to be a Husky.' I can honestly say in hindsight, it was the best decision she could have made."

The second piece was Alesha Deesing. She was the most gifted physical specimen I had ever seen. Dees was listed at six-foot-one but she played much taller. She had the ability to jump higher that everyone and then seemed to hang in the air. She was not as polished as Christal and would likely spend her freshman year learning more than playing. Everyone acknowledged that when she was ready, Dees and Darla Myhre would make a tremendous tandem as middle blockers. Until Dees was ready, junior Jessica Veris would see time in the middle.

The third player was Ashley Aratani. Ashley came from Hawaii and was a Danka clone. She was an excellent back row player, always seemed to be in the right position, and had ice water in her veins when the team needed a big serve.

The pieces seem to be in place to move from fifth in the PAC-10 to competing for the PAC-10 title and a legitimate chance to make the Final Four. There was also a sense of urgency. This would be Sanja's final season. While she was academically a junior, she was affected by an NCAA rule (I am paraphrasing it) that states a student athlete must complete their four years of eligibility before the age of twenty-five. Since Sanja was unable to start college due to the civil war in her home country until age twenty-two. She would turn twenty-five during the 2004 season. Sanja had surgery on her shoulder in the off season but appeared ready.

The team started off winning the first twelve matches. Ten of the twelve wins were 3-0 sweeps. Then, on October 4, 2004, the unimaginable occurred. The University of Washington volleyball team was ranked **number one** in the nation. The players and fans were elated. UW, once considered the Siberia of volleyball, once considered two easy wins per season for most PAC-10 schools, was the **number one** team in the land. "There is meaning in the rankings, but the real meaning is in the end," said head coach Jim McLaughlin. "The excitement is unavoidable, but you can't get too excited because you have to focus on getting better every day. The real excitement should come with our team getting better and us controlling what we can control. There are two months left to the season, and we need to be concerned with today and what we need to do to get better."

Ten days later, on October 14, the unthinkable occurred. Sanja broke her right hand in practice. The local papers reported it this way:

Tomasevic Suffers Hand Injury In Practice
Senior outside hitter will undergo surgery today

Oct. 15, 2004

SEATTLE—Washington volleyball senior outside hitter Sanja Tomasevic suffered a hand injury during practice Thursday morning and will undergo surgery today to repair displaced fractures of her third and fourth metacarpal bones. Tomasevic injured her right hand when it struck against a wall during a diving drill in the East Gym of Bank America Arena. She is expected to be sidelined for 4-5 weeks.

"I'm sad that I got hurt but this time off will allow some of my other nagging injuries to heal before the postseason," said Tomasevic. "I know I'm in good hands with my doctors and I'm anxious to heal and get back on the court. I know our team will only get stronger over the next month as different people step up and improve their games. I am confident that our team is going to continue to get better while

I am recovering because they are going to play together as a team."

Tomasevic leads the number-one-ranked Huskies in nearly every statistical category and ranks among the top three in the Pacific-10 Conference in kills, service aces and points. She was a second team All-America selection last season and has led the 2004 squad to a 13-0 overall record and 5-0 mark in the Pac-10.

The entire Husky nation's hearts sank. We were about to reach the Promised Land and our foundation, our leader, our All American, breaks her hand.

During a 2010 interview with Sanja, I asked her about the injury and her feeling at that time. "My initial reaction was 'Oh, my God, not this, not now.' We were 13-0 and ranked number one in the nation. We went through the first half of the PAC-10 season unbeaten. Next up was the Arizona schools on the road and Cal and Stanford at home. I believed we could beat the Arizona schools without me. Christal moved over to my position on the left side. Brie and Kaitlin went to the right side. Darla and Jessica Veris were solid in the middle. Candace and Danka were money on defense. Courtney still had an impressive group of attackers. The team did well without me winning ten consecutive matches."

I asked her at what point she really believed UW could win a national title. I was surprised by the answer. "I knew we could win it all while I was injured. We played Stanford at home. In the past I always put tremendous pressure on myself against Stanford. I felt that I had to have a career night for us to beat them. So Stanford comes to Seattle and we have a record crowd, nearly six thousand people. The building is electric and the team sweeps Stanford 3-0. At the end of that match I felt like a giant weight had been lifted. I don't have to have a career night for us to beat a national power. I don't have to be perfect to give us a chance. The team had arrived. The girls knew their roles and what to do and they went out and did it. I knew when I was healthy I could go with the flow of the game. I didn't have to try and force points."

This team won its first twenty-two matches. They held the number one ranking for seven weeks before a five game loss to Stanford in Palo Alto. The next night, UW beat Cal in four games to win its first ever PAC-10 championship. Sanja dressed for Stanford and Cal but saw limited action. Her broken hand was fitted with a special pad for protection. "I could not get the snap I wanted with the pad" Sanja told me later. My guess was Jim was giving her hand an extra week to heal.

I asked Sanja about the Northern California trip. "I felt I was ready and was given clearance to play. I fully expected to play and step back into my role on the left side. I mentioned that to one of the girls, and I think Jim heard me. I didn't get a lot of reps in practice but I figured, I'm an All American, I'm ready, I should play. When we went to the team meeting room, Jim would not let me in. He said I was being a selfish player and sent me back to my room. I called our trainer Suzy in tears. Her initial reaction was I reinjured my hand. Through my sobs I told her, 'He won't let me in the team meeting. He said I was selfish.' Suzy said, 'Don't worry about it. I'll bet it is just a message to the team. Besides, it will be better for your hand not to play this weekend.' Remember after the Cal game we all went to Marques' house for a little party after we beat Cal? I was still upset but I didn't say anything. When we got back to Seattle I talked to Jim and told him I was upset. He told me, 'If you don't practice well, you won't play well on the weekend. You didn't get much practice time last week. Now, if you are ready, prove it in practice. At the moment you are not one of the top two in the cauldron.' I tell you, Frank that made me so mad. I went to practice with a laser like focus. I pounded every ball. I won every drill. I didn't care who got in my way. I was going to start for the final PAC-10 weekend. Jim didn't post the stats the first few days that week. About Wednesday at the team meeting after practice, he said, 'Our All American is back. Sanja has the highest scores in UW history this week.' I realized at that moment he was sending me and everyone else a message. To me, the message was, 'We can win the PAC-10 title without any one player.' Now it was time to get ready for the tournament."

I asked Jim about this situation a few years later. He told me, "I knew Sanja was cleared to play, but that pad made it hard for her to attack the ball. I didn't want to risk aggravating the injury. Christal had been playing the left side while Sanja was out. Brie and Kaitlin were on the right side. We had won ten in a row without Sanja and I didn't want to disrupt our rhythm until Sanja had a full good week of practice. I heard her make a statement that she expected to start on the left side. Since I had already decided she would see spot action, I did not want the team to pin all its hopes on Sanja's return. What if she injured the hand again? We needed to win one in our last four league matches to become the PAC-10 Champions. I wanted the team to know it was capable of wrapping up the PAC-10 title without Sanja. I was confident we would win one of two from Stanford or Cal if not both. We were up on Stanford 2-0 then we lost our focus and dropped the next three. It was our first loss of the season. While I never want to lose, it wasn't the worst thing in the world. We won the PAC-10 the next night against Cal. The extra week of rest would help Sanja's hand. What we really needed her for was the tournament."

"So how did Sanja take this?" I asked. "She wasn't happy. She's a competitor and wanted to play. When we got back home, I told her she had to win her playing time like everyone else. We went 11-1 without her. She had to earn her way back, and she did. She had the single best week of practice of anyone during my time at UW. She was ready."

The PAC-10 season ended with the Huskies losing to USC and beating UCLA at home. Sanja was back for USC and UCLA matches. Any questions about her health were put to rest as she was named PAC-10 player of the week.

The team and fans were delighted to learn that UW would host the first and second rounds of the NCAA tournament. For the first time in over six weeks, everyone was healthy, and the Huskies were in excellent position to advance to the Final Four without leaving Seattle. Then, at Wednesday's practice, two days before the first tournament match against Idaho, Christal Morrison suffered a torn meniscus in her right knee. While the UW trainers said she was cleared to play during the postseason as she could not do further damage to the knee, her mobility and explosiveness were severely limited.

Once again the program was tested. Would they be able to operate without another key person present? They won the first two matches. Next were the regional finals in Seattle. The Huskies swept St. Mary's from Moraga, California, and then awaited the winner of the UCLA-Penn State match. With Christal injured, Penn State was far and away the favorite to win the region. Someone forgot to tell UCLA, and the Bruins upset Penn State. So it was UW and UCLA for the third time. The winner goes to the Final Four.

The POINT! HUSKIES! newsletter reported the events like this:

PAC-10 Champions and Heading to the Final Four

The magical year of firsts continues for our Huskies. Consider these firsts that our Huskies accomplished this season:

- *Champions* of the mighty PAC-10 conference.
- Ranked number one team in the nation. Our seven-week run as the number one team is the longest anyone has held the top spot.
- Averaged over 3,500 fans for each home match with a single game high of nearly 7,000.
- Hosted the NCAA regional championships in front of 9,000 of the greatest fans in the nation.
- NCAA regional champions
- **Going to the *Final Four* to play for the national title.**

Go ahead—read it again. You are not seeing things. Hell didn't freeze over and California didn't fall into the ocean. Our Huskies are *champions* of the PAC-10 and are going to the *Final Four*.

All year long we have said that the PAC-10 is the best conference in the world. This season, however, there were some whispers across the country that the PAC-10 wasn't as strong; that the PAC-10 might not get a team to the Final Four; that the rest of the country had closed the gap. For the first time no PAC-10 team was ranked the number one seed in any of the four regions. Our Huskies were ranked as the seventh seed in the tournament. Well, it is time for the rest of the nation to wake up and smell the Starbucks. **Four** of the Elite 8 and **three** of the Final Four teams are from the PAC-10.

How special has this season been? Consider this—our Huskies are 28-2 going into the Final Four. In our two loses we were in a position to win—serving for match point. If we win those two points, our Huskies are 30-0.

The 9,000 fans that attended the regional championship witnessed some of the greatest volleyball ever. UCLA defended number two Penn State 3-1, and our Huskies put on a clinic dispatching St. Mary's 3-0. This set up an All PAC-10 regional final and the third match between our Huskies and UCLA this season. The atmosphere in Bank of America Arena was electric. Our fans came early and were ready to cheer our Huskies to the Final Four. Junior outside hitter Brie Hagerty, who made the All-Tournament Team, said about the crowd, "We were talking before the match—do you feel this energy? Heck yeah, so let's get it done."

Our Huskies and UCLA played a classic match. It was the type of match that should be archived to show every aspiring volleyball player how the game is supposed to be played. The passion and intensity of the crowd was matched by that of the players. In the fifth game UCLA led 8-6 before our Huskies ripped off six straight points behind the serving of Danka Danicic and the powerful hitting of Brie Hagerty. Match point, 14-9, with the crowd in frenzy—All American Sanja Tomasevic willed her team to victory. Sanja hit three "rockets" but UCLA was able to dig and return the first two. The Bruins dug the third one and set their right outside hitter, who had a one-on-one against Sanja. Sanja "roofed" the attack and the celebration was under way. "There was no way we were going to lose in our building in front of our fans," said Sanja who was named the tournament's Most Outstanding Player. "We felt the love in the building tonight," said setter and All Tournament selection Courtney Thompson. "We won this for our fans," said Courtney.

"Wow, what a match," said head coach Jim McLaughlin. "I felt like if we just stayed in this thing, kept grinding it out, it would be a delayed gratification. And it finally came. But UCLA played well. It was just an unbelievable match."

Yes, coach, it was an unbelievable match, and now our Huskies are champions of the PAC-10 and going to the Final Four to play for the national title. Go ahead—read it again.

So it was back to Long Beach, but this time it was with the chance to win the national title. The opponent for the third time in one year was Stanford. The teams split the first two games, then Stanford's All American, Ogonna Nnamani, imposed her will, and the season ended losing 3-1.

The boosters, donors, fans, and parents were delighted. Four years ago there was a better chance that California would actually fall into the ocean than the University of Washington volleyball would reach the Final Four. The players, however, were devastated. "I didn't have my best game tonight," said Courtney. "We know we are better than Stanford, we just didn't show it when it counted." For Sanja, the loss was bittersweet. "I am proud of my career here in Washington, but I am disappointed that I won't be on the court when we win the national title."

UW submitted to the NCAA a hardship appeal on Sanja's behalf for an additional year of eligibility. A decision was expected in May 2005. While the odds were not in her favor, Sanja continued to work out alone. "Jim told me it was a long shot for us to win the appeal. He didn't want me to work out in the spring with the team because he did not want to build up the hope that I might return. I understood and agreed completely, so I did everything the running, hitting, weight training by myself. I planned for the worst but prayed for the best." Finally, on May 5, 2005, the NCAA issued the following ruling:

> Washington volleyball player Sanja Tomesevic will return for a fourth season of competition next fall. Under NCAA eligibility rules, Tomasevic was penalized a year of eligibility because of her late enrollment in college. The NCAA recently granted an eligibility petition filed by UW on Tomasevic's behalf, thereby awarding her a fourth year of competition.
>
> The NCAA granted the waiver based on a variety of circumstances beyond Tomasevic's control that delayed her ability to enroll in college. Primarily among those circumstances was the 1999 war between NATO and her home country of Yugoslavia.

The POINT! HUSKIES! newsletter reported it this way:

She's BAAAACK!!!! Sanja Receives a 4th Year of Eligibility

That loud noise recently heard from the Northwest was not an earthquake or a massive thunder storm, or any other natural disaster. That noise was the sound every Husky volleyball fan jumping up and wildly cheering for Sanja Tomasevic. The NCAA (yes, that NCAA) has granted Sanja a fourth year of eligibility. The NCAA granted the waiver based on a variety of circumstances beyond Sanja's control that delayed her ability to enroll in college. Primarily among those circumstances was the 1999 war between NATO and her home country of Yugoslavia.

"Sanja has been an integral part of our team for the past three years and she has helped us build the program to where it stands currently," said Jim McLaughlin. "Having missed a good part of last season due to injury, I am very pleased that she will get another chance to show everyone what kind of player she is." "This is awesome," said assistant coach Leslie Tuiasosopo. "Sanja works so hard and to lose most of last season to a broken hand was heartbreaking." All American setter Courtney Thompson said, "This is great news. I can't wait for the season to begin."

"I am so grateful for this opportunity" said Sanja. "I came to UW because I want to be on the court when we win our first national championship. We came so close last year— now it is time to take care of business." Maybe that loud noise was the rest of the country wailing and gnashing their teeth when they heard the news.

Last season our Huskies gave us a year to remember. Let's take one last stroll down memory lane:

- Jim McLaughlin was named PAC-10 coach of the year for the second time in three years and national coach of the year. The entire country finally recognized what we have known all along—that Jim McLaughlin is the best at what he does.
- Three Huskies named to the All American Team. Junior Candace Lee, sophomore Courtney Thompson, and freshman Christal Morrison are All Americans, and each one is coming back next season. An NCAA rule that a player must participate in 60 percent of his or her team's games is the reason Sanja was not also honored. (Note: That rule has since been changed. Even missing twelve games with a broken hand, Sanja would still have been an All American selection by the coaches.)
- Four Huskies named to All Pacific Region Team. Juniors Brie Hagerty and Candace Lee, sophomore Courtney Thompson, and freshman Christal Morrison were selected to this elite group.
- Five Huskies named to the All PAC-10 team: juniors Brie Hagerty, Candace Lee, and Darla Myhre, sophomore Courtney Thompson, and freshman Christal Morrison.
- Five Huskies named to the PAC-10 All Academic team: seniors Sanja Tomasevic (3.34), and Kaitlin Leck (3.06), juniors Candace Lee (3.78) and Danka Danicic (3.42),

and sophomore Courtney Thompson (3.63). Our Huskies epitomize the term "student/athlete."

- Two Huskies named ESPN All Academic All Americans, junior Candace Lee and sophomore Courtney Thompson.
- PAC-10 champions.
- Ranked number one team in the nation. Our seven-week run as the number one team is the longest anyone held the top spot.
- Averaged over 3,500 fans for each home match with a single game high of 7,000.
- Hosted the NCAA regional championships in front of 9,000 of the greatest fans in the nation.
- NCAA regional champions.
- **Final Four.**

The memories will stay with us forever—but last year is over and it is time to turn our attention to the upcoming season. As reigning PAC-10 champions, our Huskies will have a target on their back. They will be ready for the challenge. "We intend to defend our PAC-10 title, go to the Final Four again, and this time bring the national championship trophy back to Seattle" said Sanja. "We have experience and depth at every position," said All American Courtney Thompson. "We are not satisfied just making it to the Final Four. We want to be national champions." **Stay tuned for another terrific season**.

Chapter 10

TURN-AROUND RULE #8—REVIEW ALL ASPECTS OF THE ORGANIZATION AND MAKE ADJUSTMENTS AS NEEDED TO STAY ON COURSE

* * *

The one constant I found in my professional career was change. Every business or organization does some things well and other things not so well. As a leader, my job is to change the things we did well to make them better and have the courage to eliminate the things we didn't do well. It also means changing or adding new products or services to increase revenue and improve profit. Dr. Alfred E. Osbourne from the Anderson School of Business at UCLA once told me, "If you are not changing, then you are not growing. If you are not growing, then you are dying." Truly great leaders constantly evaluate themselves. They have the diligence to look into future and project how their business or organization will fare in the market. Once they have a good sense of what the market is doing and what opportunities the market is offering, they must have the courage to change.

Jim Collins, in *Good to Great*, wrote about Charles R. "Cork" Walgreen, the CEO of Walgreen's Drug Stores. At one point Walgreen's food service (soda fountain) business was highly profitable. When Mr. Walgreen projected into the future, he saw there was no role for the soda fountain concept. Convenient locations and wide product availability were the keys to success. While many people thought he was crazy, within five years, five hundred Walgreen's soda fountains restaurants were removed. Walgreen's stores appeared at busy intersections and profits soared.

I experienced the need for a major change several times in my turn-around management career. At the time I met Dr. Osbourne, the company I was with sold computer equipment, predominately Sun Microsystems, to large telephone companies. In the early days, profit margins were good, so the company did not develop its technical talent to offer high-margin professional services. I was brought in at a time when hardware margins had fallen to the low single-digit level. Continuing with the same business model would lead to failure. A major change was needed. We won a small service contract to develop a monitoring system for BellSouth's telephone switches. The project was funded as part of the Atlanta Olympics. I spent a large amount of time in Atlanta, Alabama, and Florida, and became very close to a top-notch BellSouth technical team.

Shortly after the Olympics, BellSouth, like many of the other regional Bells, was planning a reduction in force through a voluntary retirement. I was in Birmingham, Alabama, at a meeting with the three top BellSouth technical team leaders. I made a proposition to them, asking what their feelings were about the voluntary retirement program. They said, "It's too bad, because it's the good people who usually leave. They get a very good severance package and have another job in a month making more money. The people who stay are the ones you want to leave."

I asked if their positions would be eligible for the package, and they all said yes. I told them, "I want to set up a professional services division. We have a shot at two projects we could win very soon overseas with AT&T. There are several others we could win if I had this division. I want the three of you to head it up. It could be based here in Birmingham. You would report to me, but I want you to drive this business. If you take the BellSouth package on a Friday, you'll be on my payroll the next Monday. Think about it." A few days later, I received a call that all three were very interested. We closed the deal in less than a week, and a professional services division was born. It was a huge risk. The company was stepping far outside its comfort zone, but I kept hearing the words from Dr. Osbourne: "If you are not changing, then you are not growing. If you are not growing, then you are dying." We won more than $5 million in high-margin service deals in the next twelve months.

* * *

While, the 2004 season had brought the University of Washington's volleyball program its greatest success, Jim McLaughlin and the team knew adjustments and changes were necessary to win the national title. Assistant coach Pat Stangle left for the head coaching job at the University of Wyoming. Jose "Keno" Gandara joined Leslie Tuiasosopo as assistant coach. Jim felt that to reach the next level, team defense, particularly blocking at the net, was the key. Keno's specialty was coaching the block. "As good as our back row is with Candace, Danka, and Ashley, who dig everything, if we can just get a touch on more balls, we will win more points," said Jim. "This is what Keno will bring."

Another huge change was looming. Sophomore Alesha Deesing was ready to bring her considerable talent to the forefront. Dees spend her freshman year practicing, watching, and learning. She had the potential to be a monster blocking on defense. She could also dominate with Darla on the quick set and could run the "slide" to the outside better than anyone in the nation. The emergence of Dees meant Final Four starter Jessica Veris' playing time would be limited. "Jessica didn't sulk or complain," said Sanja. "She just worked harder and harder in practice and pushed both Darla and Dees to become better. Jess knew the national championship is a team accomplishment, and the better we were in practice, the better our chances." Every organization needs a Jessica Veris.

With the news that Sanja would be back, the team trained with a singleness of purpose. Practices were like small wars. No one gave an inch and everyone improved. Mike Morrison, Christal's father, once told me, "I watched practice one day and it was like a who's who of volleyball. There were four All Americans and two more All PAC-10 players going at it. If they can stay healthy, this could be the year."

Four more of the right people came onto the bus. Three freshmen Jessica Swarbrick, Jill Collymore, and Tamari Miyashiro, plus transfer Stevie Mussie, joined the program. While they didn't see much playing time in 2005, they brought a high level of skill and intensity to practice. All three would make their mark in the future.

I had never seen an athletic team so focused. The 2005 team demanded excellence. They expected to win. They started with season 12-0, all 3-0 sweeps, including back-to-back sweeps against Hawaii on the road. Cal took them to five games and Stanford to four before both fell. The team was 14-0 with the LA teams coming to town. After dismantling both 3-0, a UCLA fan said to me, "I thought your team last year was the best I ever saw. But this year's team is light-years better. They have the eyes of an assassin. They are so good it's scary. They don't even do a big celebration after they win. It's like they expect to dominate you."

UW was ranked number two in the nation. Halfway across the country, the University of Nebraska had staked a claim to the number one ranking. Nebraska, a two-time National Champion whose last title was in 2000, had missed the Final Four in 2004, and they were not happy. They set the national title as their 2005 goal and had the fire power to make it happen, including four of their own All Americans.

Both teams matched wins at 22-0. UW went into Pauley Pavilion to meet UCLA. They had swept USC the night before, but the team seems sluggish as the match began. UCLA had a huge and very loud crowd. A UCLA win would be number one thousand for Coach Andy Banachowski. UCLA won the first two games. The Huskies regrouped at the break and won games three and four. It was the fourth time this season they were pushed to a fifth game. UCLA kept scratching and clawing and pulled off the upset with a 15-13 fifth-game win. The UCLA fans and team reacted as if they just won the national title. Coach Banachowski was given the "Gatorade shower" and the Huskies' dream of an unbeaten season ended. "We were so upset after the match" said Sanja. "There was no way we should have lost. We weren't focused enough. As bad as we felt, we knew we learned a critical lesson. We had to bring our 'A' game every night. Jim had to build time off for us to rest into our practice schedule because all the players raised the intensity level in practice after the loss. We didn't care about the rankings at that moment. We set a goal of perfection for the rest of the season. We were not going to lose another game the rest of the year."

With the UW loss, Nebraska strengthened its grip on the number one spot. Penn State moved into number two, and UW dropped to number three. Nebraska continued to roll to 28-0. Their last match before the tournament was against conference rival and number-eleven-ranked Texas on the road. Nebraska had swept Texas forty-five days earlier, but that Thanksgiving weekend- Texas ended Nebraska's perfect season 3-2.

Nebraska would stay home for the first and second rounds of the NCAA tournament. They would travel to nearby Omaha for the regional championships. UW was sent packing to Colorado for rounds one and two, then to College Station, Texas, for the regional finals. The Final Four would be in San Antonio. With final exams coming between the regional finals and the Final Four, it looked like the UW team would have to leave College Station, Texas, on Sunday morning, return to Seattle for final exams Monday and Tuesday, then fly back to San Antonio, Texas, Tuesday night. The Washington provost, however, allowed the team to stay in Texas and have the final exams e-mailed to the Westin Hotel in San Antonio. A university official would proctor the final exams for the team. When I spoke to the proctor after the exams were completed, he told me, "It was a very easy decision. Coach McLaughlin has graduated every player in his program, and the team carries the highest GPA of all our athletic teams." So the Huskies stayed in Texas between the regional finals and the Final Four. They were able to schedule some fun and attend the filming of the television show *Extreme Makeover: Home Edition* in Washington, Texas. How ironic.

The experts (people who just read press clipping) predicted Nebraska, UW, and Penn State would be Final Four shoo-ins. Penn State lost, but Nebraska and UW swept every opponent in route to San Antonio. Legions of Nebraska "Big Red" fans descended on San Antonio. They had busloads of fans. In fact, Nebraska's overflow was put into the Westin with the few hundred Husky fans and team. Everywhere you looked on the River Walk, you saw red. According to the paper, it was a foregone conclusion that Nebraska would win the national title. The movie *King Kong* had just been released. One local paper ran a cartoon with King

Kong on the Empire State Building in a red jersey holding the national championship trophy with Nebraska's name on the trophy. The UW fans and players found it amusing but said nothing. I heard comments from a few Nebraska fans: "Well, we just hope you give us a good match." My response was, "I wouldn't worry about that." One of the local papers carried a quote that was attributed to Sanja that said, "We will crush them." The few less-than-cordial Nebraska fans made it a point to mention that: "we'll see who gets crushed."

"Yes, we will," I replied.

UW drew Tennessee, while Nebraska took on a Cinderella team, Santa Clara. Both made short work of their opponents, and the showdown was set between Nebraska and Washington to face off for all the marbles. As I spent time at the hotels and the All American banquet, there was an interesting undertone. I kept hearing coaches say Washington was going to win. Their reasons were that UW had superior numbers in every major category; Washington was returning their entire team that made the Final Four in 2004; and the PAC-10 was a much tougher league. Nebraska, while very good, was not as experienced and had not made the Final Four in 2004. One coach went as far to whisper, "Washington is going to win, and it won't even be close." I have to admit, even though I believed UW would win, I was surprised by what I heard.

Well, Saturday night, December 17, 2005, finally arrived. The Nebraska fans had us outnumbered about seven thousand to three hundred. Nonetheless, there was optimism among the Husky faithful. I asked Sanja, "How was the preparation for Nebraska?" She answered, "We were confident we would win. The first night Jim showed us film of Nebraska crushing someone. We left the meeting to go to bed, and I have to admit I was a little concerned. I said to Brie and Danka, 'They looked awful good.' Danka said, 'It is part of Jim's plan. He doesn't want us overconfident.' Then he succeeded. The next night we watched film of Nebraska's loss to Texas, and I believed we would win. Finally, Jim said, 'Remember the film at the All American Banquet where they showed all four teams winning their region?

Tennessee, Santa Clara, and Nebraska all celebrated like they had accomplished their goal. When you walked off the court after beating Wisconsin, there was no wild celebration. Every one of you held up two fingers. You acknowledged that there was more to accomplish. Two more wins to get. I knew right there we were going to win.'"

Sanja continued, "When we went onto the court, I was shocked at the size of Nebraska. They looked like giants and I felt like a little midget. Then I looked around the arena and saw all that red and a little spot of purple. I thought, 'Oh, my God.' Then Jim called us all in and said, 'Hey, we are over here. Focus on what we are doing here.' We continued our preparation and were ready for the match to begin."

Just before the match started, Nebraska's large inflatable Husker mascot sprung a leak and completely deflated. All of the UW fans hoped that was a sign of things to come. The time for talking was over. I asked Sanja, "At what point in the match did you know you had it?" She said, "Courtney Thompson served an ace for the first point of game one. The next point Darla and I stuffed Nebraska's first attack. It was 2-0 and Nebraska called time out. We went back to our huddle and I said, 'It's over—they're ours!'"

The Huskies won the first two games. The UW fans were cautiously optimistic. We all figured Nebraska would come out strong in game three and then we would win game four. Nebraska did come out strong in game three, holding leads of 7-2, 16-12 and 23-22. Once UW tied the match at 23 each, I knew it was over. Game three was a 30-26 UW win. Mighty Nebraska had been swept and the University of Washington was the national champion.

The POINT! HUSKIES! newsletter reported the following:

NATIONAL CHAMPIONS

From the first day Coach Jim McLaughlin arrived at UW we said it was only a matter of when, not if, our Huskies would be national champions. The "when" happened last weekend! Our Huskies traveled to San Antonio for their second consecutive trip to the Final Four. From the accounts in the San Antonio papers and TV, this was supposed to be a coronation for Nebraska. The other three teams were simply invited to attend. Unfortunately, someone forgot to tell our Huskies.

Our Huskies came on the floor with a fire and determination that would not be denied. The tone was set after the first two points of game one. Courtney served an ace, then Darla and Sanja "roofed" Nebraska's first attack. With the score 2-0, Nebraska called time out. They appeared stunned and our Huskies never let them recover. Husky bodies were flying all over the court, digging everything Nebraska could muster. Candace showed again why she is the "All World Libero." "We were one step ahead of them the entire match," said Sanja. "All we heard for the past three months is 'Nebraska is huge, they're big, and they're King Kong.' We couldn't wait for this match to begin. We knew we would win."

Our Huskies beat mighty Nebraska 3-0. It was total domination in every aspect of the game. Our Huskies out blocked, out hit, out dug, out served, and out coached Nebraska. "Our goal all year was the national championship," said Courtney. "We weren't going to back down."

In bringing the first ever volleyball national championship to UW, Jim McLaughlin accomplished what *no one* has ever done—win a national title as the head coach of a women's and men's program. "When I moved from coaching men to women, I was told that you can't teach women the men's style of volleyball," said Jim. "I never believed that. Volleyball is volleyball—gender doesn't matter." Well, coach, now the entire country knows two things that we already knew— Jim McLaughlin is the best volleyball coach, period, and our Huskies are the best team in the nation.

Sadly we say thank you and good-bye to our seniors— Sanja Tomasevic, Brie Hagerty, Candace Lee, Darla Myhre, Danka Danicic, Jessica Veris, and Carolyn Farney. These young women were Jim McLaughlin's first recruiting class.

What these women accomplished in four years is truly remarkable. They will go down in Husky history as the first senior class to play in the NCAA tournament four consecutive years, including one Elite 8 and the Final Four twice. They brought our program to the elite status. They brought out record crowds to watch volleyball. They gave us pride in Husky volleyball. They built the foundation for years of success. They brought us the national championship. *We will never forget you.*

Thank you to all the POINT! HUSKIES! fans and donors for your unconditional support. Programs don't win national championships without your help. Please take a minute and send a donation to the volleyball program. Our Huskies brought us the national championship—now it's our turn.

Sophomore Christal Morrison was named the Final Four's most outstanding player. Nebraska appeared to be overcompensating toward Sanja. Sanja told me, "They had to over compensate because of our plan. Jim didn't have me pass the Nebraska serve. He told me, 'I want you to completely focus on attacking.' Since I wasn't receiving the serve, I was always ready to attack. I could see Nebraska looking at me, and Christal and Brie made them pay." Christal scored the final point on a block that set off a wild and spontaneous celebration on the court. UW players and fans were delirious while the Nebraska faithful were in shock. The celebration moved from the court to a restaurant on the River Walk. The team arrived carrying the national championship trophy, singing Queen's song "We Are the Champions" over and over. Washington President Mark Emmert addressed the jubilant crowd and announced the University of Washington volleyball was so dominant in this tournament that they were the first team to sweep every opponent since the field was expanded to sixty-four teams. I stood off to the side and took in the celebration. In August 2001, I met Jim McLaughlin. He was taking over one of the worst programs I had ever seen, and now, December 17, 2005, the University of Washington ruled the volleyball world. As the celebration calmed down, Jim called me over and handed me the national championship trophy. He said, "Here—I promised you four years ago you would hold this." I held the trophy with tears in my eyes. Several of the players hugged me. It is a moment I will never forget. The celebration then moved to a place called Howl at the Moon, where the team and supporters danced until the wee hours of the morning.

After what seemed to be fifteen minutes of sleep, I was at the airport. I bought the local paper, which had a picture at the moment the ball hit the floor. The picture could have been titled "Elation." I still have that picture in a frame in my office. It will be something I cherish forever.

The changes Jim had the courage to make before the 2005 season worked. Keno, who was brought in to improve the block, excelled. The 2005 team achieved their greatest number of blocks per game in nearly ten years (3.13). Three Huskies averaged more than one block per game, including All PAC-10 player Darla Myhre, All American Alesha Deesing, and All American, PAC-10 player of the year and Asics national player of the year Sanja Tomasevic.

The second major change was inserting Alesha Deesing as middle blocker. All she did was become an All American and, together with Darla Myhre, the best blocking tandem in the country. Now before you volleyball purists start pulling out statistics to challenge me, answer this: which two middle blockers were holding the national championship trophy on December 17, 2005? Enough said!

The third major change was moving Sanja from the left to the right side. This put sophomore Christal Morrison as the primary left-side attacker. "I was vilified on the volleyball blogs," said Jim McLaughlin. "I read things like 'McLaughlin has lost what little of his mind he has left. He made the Final Four, and then moves his best player to the right side. Maybe the lack of sunshine in Seattle has warped his brain.' I knew it was a gamble, but teams prepare their defense for the left-side hitter. With Sanja on the right side, it meant teams could not load up on

Christal. They had to respect Sanja, and this gave Christal and Brie more one-on-one opportunities." Well, coach, the lack of sun didn't warp your brain too badly, since the only person with the national championship trophy, the coach of the year award, and the only coach to ever win the national title with a men's and women's program is you!

Chapter 11

TURN-AROUND RULE #9—CONTINUE TO BRING IN PEOPLE THAT ARE BETTER THAN THE ONES ALREADY IN PLACE.

* * *

I have heard people ask, "After you have achieved success, how are you going to find people better than what you have?" I always answer this way: "I constantly continue to raise the bar. If I am successful, then my business or organization has grown. As I grow, I look for more of the right people to join the organization and continue to replace average people who have left with the right people."

Selecting people is not an exact science. You can create a profile; run background checks; perform tests like Myers/Briggs; do handwriting analysis; conduct drug tests; check references; you name it and there is a test for it. Unfortunately, there is still a degree of "hit or miss" when selecting staff. I found that after I do some of the aforementioned steps, I have a face-to-face meeting. I talk about the challenges the business or organization faces. I talk about the successes we had and where we hope and plan to go. I talk about our vision. What I am looking for is the person to engage; to become involved in the conversation; someone who can both express and envision himself or herself achieving the vision. I often try to ascertain how people have dealt with a difficult or challenging situation. I listen to see if they make excuses or look to pass the blame. I fully believe that difficult times don't build character; difficult times reveal character. People of strong character excel during difficult or challenging situations. They talk about how they learned and grew and improved during hard times. They don't quit or look for a scapegoat. They dig in and work harder. They find a way.

I also look in their eyes. The right people have a fire in their eyes. Their eyes widen as they talk about their goals and abilities. Their eyes often give me a tip if they are the right person. Once again, it is not an exact science.

* * *

For the UW volleyball program and every other collegiate athletic program, change is inevitable. It is called graduation. Every year some players graduate or leave the program. Every season has a new team. The 2006 season was a major change. As the reigning national and back-to-back PAC-10 champions, the Huskies were the hunted. Gone was the amazing first recruiting class that took the program from worst in the PAC-10 to the national title, but the cupboard was far from bare. The team was lead by senior All American setter Courtney Thompson. Courtney simply willed her team to win. She refused to lose. She was without question the hardest-working player in the nation. Courtney was joined by All Americans Christal Morrison and Alesha Deesing. Sophomore Jessica Swarbrick was expected to be the second middle. The huge holes were who would play opposite Christal, libero and defensive specialist. Junior transfer Stevie Mussie and senior transfer Janine Sandell won the outside spot. Redshirt freshman Tamari Miysahiro would step in for the legendary Candace Lee, and newcomer Megan McAfee would join Ashley Aratani in the Danka role. The physically gifted Becky Perry would redshirt. UW made a very strong recruiting run at Megan Hodge but lost to Penn State. Several new people were going to have to find a way for UW to earn its third consecutive trip to the Final Four.

The preseason polls figured that even with three returning All Americans, UW had lost too much, and they ranked the Huskies number three in the PAC-10. "The only poll that matters is the last one," said Courtney Thompson. The team finished the pre-PAC-10 season 10-1, the only loss being a five-game match against highly ranked Texas. They swept Stanford and Cal but then lost back-to-back matches in LA to UCLA and USC. Based on the sheer will of Courtney Thompson, UW ran off another twelve consecutive wins before losing to Stanford on the road. Courtney was on the way to becoming the all-time PAC-10 assist leader, and Christal Morrison was taking aim on Sanja's career records for kills and points. Despite a 25-5 season record, second-place finish in the PAC-10, and the number three ranking in the country, UW was seeded number six for the 2006 team NCAA Tournament. The general sentiment was UW had a great season given how much they lost to graduation; but there was no way the team could make the Final Four for the third straight season.

The 2006 NCAA tournament saw the Huskies going back to Colorado, where they uncharacteristically took four games each to dispatch Colorado State and Colorado. Next was their fourth consecutive trip to the regional finals. The difference this year was that the regional finals were in Seattle. Three Big-10 teams—Ohio State, Purdue, and Penn State—were coming to Seattle. Penn State, the number three seed in the tournament, was the prohibitive favorite. Penn State's last trip to Seattle was during the 2004 regional final. They were also the prohibitive favorite then, but lost to UCLA. UW then defeated UCLA to earn its first trip to the Final Four. In 2006, Penn State was on a mission. It appeared they were sent back to Seattle to redeem themselves for losing the 2004. Penn State drew conference rival Purdue, whom they quickly defeated. UW, in turn, swept Ohio State, which set up the match everyone wanted to see back in 2004: UW vs. Penn State, with the winner going to the Final Four.

This match would provide far more drama than usual. It would feature Christal Morrison, the PAC-10 player of the year, vs. Megan Hodge, the Big-10 player of the year. Penn State had secured freshman Megan Hodge, who was also highly coveted by UW. This would be her first trip to Seattle since her official visit. The UW fans did not forget the snub. The noise at Bank of America Arena was deafening as 6,549 fans drowned out the public address announcer. UW won the first two games, which made the crowd more delirious with excitement. Penn State won game three 30-28, then Courtney said to her teammates, "This ends with game four." She was right.

A new star was born during game four. Redshirt freshman Tamari (Tama) Miyashiro, who replaced the legend Candace Lee as libero, fueled the Washington comeback with a stellar defensive performance which forced the game into long rallies where Washington felt it had the advantage. Her eighteen digs led the Huskies and brought her just twenty-nine digs away from tying the school record for a single season. Let's look at that last line again. A redshirt freshman was close to breaking the single season record for digs set by the great Candace Lee. The greatest libero in the history of the college game was replaced by someone who would be even better. "Tama is a freshman, and the influence she has on our team is unbelievable," McLaughlin said. "She's the best volleyball player I've ever coached in every way, shape, and form. She made some very good plays."

Tama and the entire Washington defense was the key in holding Big-10 player and freshman of the year Megan Hodge in check. Hodge, who hit .429 against Purdue, did have seventeen kills, but she also had fifteen errors to hit just .039.

"We thought it was a key match-up to get on her," McLaughlin said. "We felt like if we could get to her tendencies we wouldn't stop her, but we would slow her down a bit. And we did that." Christal Morrison was more than ready for the showdown. UW fans noticed a fair amount of "dialogue" between Christal and Megan Hodge. When I asked Christal about some of the dialogue, she said with a smile, "I just wanted her to know which team was going to be watching the Final Four on television."

The crowd was so loud and so excited and so much a factor in this win that following the match, senior Courtney Thompson led her team around the edge of the floor and then into the stands to celebrate with the crowd, which gave the team a nearly ten-minute ovation. It was a moment I will never forget. The win marked the thirty-first-straight victory for the Huskies at home, a program record, and their tenth NCAA tournament win in a row. Washington had won thirty of thirty-three games in that ten-match span.

Of course, the POINT! HUSKIES! newsletter had its own unique spin on the third consecutive trip to the Final Four.

WOW Final Four Again

Let's talks about things that happen at UW every December. First there are final exams. This is usually not traumatic for the volleyball program, which has graduated every player and holds a GPA in the 3.4 range. Then there is Christmas and the Christmas break—time that all Huskies enjoy. Husky volleyball has started a new December tradition—going to the *Final Four*.

For the third consecutive year our Huskies are headed to the *Final Four*. Three consecutive years—no other team in the tournament can make that claim. For many schools, getting to the *Final Four* once is the highlight of their program. These schools have one great team that has one great season. When you make the *Final Four* in three consecutive years, you have a great program, not one great season. Jim McLaughlin has built a great program—six consecutive NCAA tournaments, four consecutive years to the Elite 8, and three consecutive trips to the *Final Four*. He has a roadmap that he reviews with every recruit. He talks about standards. He can point to UW players who have become far better than anyone expected. He talks about the Husky experience and how a recruit can fit into the program. He accepts only those student-athletes who are willing to commit to the program. Great individual talent but an unwillingness to fit into the system will not get a student-athlete into this program. As Courtney Thompson has said, "Everything Jim told me has happened."

The model is simple to discuss but difficult to execute. How many programs in any sport immediately come to mind? I can think of John Wooden at UCLA, Red Auerbach's Boston Celtics, and Phil Jackson's Chicago Bulls. All were programs led by tremendous coaches with a plan; coaches who could make players understand the sum is greater than the individual parts; coaches who are champions. Coaches like Jim McLaughlin.

So our Huskies are off to Omaha to meet our old friend Stanford in the semifinals. Each team won handily on their home court. Now we'll see what happens on a neutral court. According to the experts, the winner will play Nebraska (although UCLA may have something to say about that) for the national title. Stanford and Nebraska were preseason picks to make the FINAL FOUR. The experts did not include our Huskies. We talked about that in our last issue—but we're baaack.

With only two graduating seniors, there is an excellent chance our Huskies would be in Sacramento next December for their fourth consecutive *Final Four*. So remember to update your calendars every December:

- Final exams
- Christmas break
- Husky volleyball in the *Final Four*

So the Husky fans packed up our things and flew to Omaha Nebraska for the Final Four. Nebraska had spent the entire year as number one, and they were still smarting from the 2005 loss to UW. As we walked around Omaha, the Nebraska faithful gave us our respect as the reigning champions but quickly added, "We hope we get to play you again for the title." My response was simply, "So do I." Stanford, however, crashed the party and swept our Huskies 3-0. Nebraska went on to easily defeat Stanford and win the national title in front of their home crowd. As I watched the celebration, I hoped that someday UW would host and win the Final Four volleyball in Seattle. It would be a fitting tribute to the people of Seattle, who have supported and meant so much to this program.

The awards continued to come for the UW players. Four University of Washington volleyball players have received All-America honors. Senior setter Courtney Thompson and junior outside hitter Christal Morrison were first-team picks, while junior middle blocker Alesha Deesing was a second-team honoree and sophomore middle blocker Jessica Swarbrick was a third-team selection. Washington and Nebraska were the only teams to have four players earn All-America honors.

The Huskies, who have earned nineteen All-America awards, have won eleven in the last three seasons and thirteen since head coach Jim McLaughlin took over the program in 2001. Eleven of Washington's honorees have been first-team selections.

The awards didn't stop there for Courtney Thompson. She became the first UW student-athlete to win the Honda-Broderick Cup, which is awarded annually to the collegiate woman athlete of the year.

Courtney, Washington's only three-time first-team All-American and two-time Academic All-American, led Washington to its third consecutive national semifinal and closed out her career as one of the most decorated Huskies in program's history.

She set the Pacific-10 Conference record with 6,552 career assists, which ranks third on the NCAA all-time list. She also set the NCAA record with 14.56 assists per game and became just the second player in PAC-10 history to amass six thousand career assists.

The young woman whom every major program said was "too slow, too short, and didn't have good enough hands" was the collegiate woman athlete of the year. She was also named to the U.S. national team and was among six recipients of the Seattle Storm's WNBA second annual "Women of Inspiration" award. The honorees are women who are leaders in their respective fields and pioneers of women in their positions. Courtney has gone on the play professionally in Puerto Rico, Switzerland, and Spain, plus may well represent the United States in the 2012 Olympics. While Sanja will forever be revered as the foundation of this program, Courtney will forever be the heart and soul.

The UW supporters again showed their generosity by donating $40,000 to the program. The University of Washington volleyball program was now among the best in the nation. UW volleyball matches became an event. UW led the PAC-10 in attendance and was in the top five in the nation the past four years.

When the Huskies went on the road, their opponents often had their largest crowd of the year. The players were acknowledged and recognized around campus. Jim's summer camps sold out in twenty minutes. In five years, this program went to the Elite 8 and three consecutive Final Fours. A player from the 2001 team said to me, "The transformation of this program happened so quickly it is beyond belief. Most of the girls I played with in 2001 would not make the team now."

＊ ＊ ＊

Chapter 12

TURN-AROUND RULE #10—THE LEADER CANNOT LOSE SIGHT OF THE GOAL

* * *

As a business leader, the worst thing you can do is relax when your business or organization is doing well. Maybe it had to do with growing up in a hard luck town outside of Buffalo, New York, but when things are going well, I find myself working harder to continue the success. My friends and family use to tell me to "sit back and enjoy what you have accomplished." I tried, but something in the back of my mind kept telling me, "If what I am doing is successful, it won't be long before everyone else figures it out." We have to work harder to see where the market is going; to make sure we are reacting quickly enough to market trends and condition. I was always taught and still believe that whatever the market conditions are that put us in a good place, those conditions were going to change. If I wasn't constantly looking to indentify that change and have a plan to address the change, the good times would be a distant memory. Many executives have told me they are more nervous when things are going well.

I can't recall the speaker's name at a turn-around management conference I attended in New Orleans, but I will never forget what he said. "We worked so hard to pull our company from the brink of disaster. We were able to convince the staff that we had the right plan and the right vision. Everyone was on the same page at the same time. As things started to improve, I noticed complacency had begun. The attention to detail was not as intense. Our people started to relax and fall back into some bad habits. As a result, things starting failing through the cracks. I saw it, but I guess I started to believe our own press releases and didn't move quickly enough, and we found ourselves back in danger."

I have a *Successories* picture in my office that I look at and read every day. The picture is the face of a tiger, camouflaged by brush, stalking its next meal. The caption reads: "*Change*. In today's world there are two kinds of companies…the quick and the dead!" It serves as a reminder every day to "not lose sight of the goal."

∗ ∗ ∗

After three consecutive Final Fours, UW fans were a little spoiled. We almost had the feeling that the Final Four was our birthright or something that was supposed to happen. There was reason for the optimism. After all, we had four returning All Americans. Senior Christal Morrison would certainly surpass the great Sanja Tomasevic as the all time UW leader in kills, attacks, and points. She would also become the program's first four-time All American. The middle blocker position was solid with two returning All Americans, senior Alesha Deesing and junior Jessica Swarbrick. Sophomore libero Tama Miyashiro was not only an All American; she was also the national defensive player of the year. Senior Stevie Mussie, the incredibly athletic redshirt freshman Becky Perry, and explosive freshman Kindra Carlson would round out the front line. Joining Tama in the back row were senior Ashley Aratani and sophomore Megan McAfee. Given the depth in the front line, Jill Collymore would redshirt this season. Airial Salvo, a transfer from Utah, would also redshirt. The big question mark was setter. True freshman Jenna Hagglund would run the offense.

The experts didn't give this team a lot of love, ranking them number eight in the preseason polls. At the preseason team scrimmage, Jim McLaughlin said to me, "We are so young at so many places this year. I think we are a good team. We are going to have to grow up fast. We'll see if we can become a great team." The team started the year like it wanted to become a great team, winning its first sixteen matches. Fourteen of the sixteen wins were 3-0. At the halfway point of the PAC-10 season, things were looking good. The POINT! HUSKIES! newsletter reported the following:

Tied for First Place Halfway Through the PAC-10

Image for a moment you are a head coach. You look at your schedule and see that in the next seven days you will play four teams ranked in the *top 10* in the *nation*. Even worse, these four teams are all in your conference, and three of them are ranked higher than you. OK—you can stop shaking. It was just pretend. You say to yourself, "*No one* gets a schedule like that." No one except Coach Jim McLaughlin and the 2007 Huskies.

Our Huskies started this nightmarish week with a disappointing five-game loss to number ten Cal. Tired, disappointed, and frustrated, our Huskies crossed the San Francisco Bay to meet "mighty" Stanford the next night. Stanford was ranked number two in the nation. They were undefeated and had swept our Huskies the last two times we played. Over three thousand Stanford faithful were expecting the streak to continue. Stanford was ahead two games to one and leading in game four. Maples Pavilion was rocking. Then our Huskies came back to life. It was like watching Dr. Bruce Banner become the Incredible Hulk (boy, am I dating myself). Our All Americans Christal Morrison, Jessica Swarbrick, and Alesha Deesing played like All Americans. Joined by senior Stevie Mussie and two freshmen, Becky Perry and Kindra Carlson, our Huskies battled back to win game four. Stanford took the lead in game five 8-7—but sophomore libero Tamari Miyashiro's "flying digs" kept us in the game. With the lead at 13-10, sophomore Megan McAfee served an *ace* that hit the tape of the net, then, as if we were watching in slow motion, the ball crawled up the tape and over the net for point number 14. You could see the air come out of the Stanford players. The next play, freshman Jenna Hagglund set Christal in the back row for a monster kill. There is nothing like the sound of three thousand screaming Stanford fans and the band going suddenly *silent*.

"It was an interesting two days. We didn't play to our standards against Cal. We lost our intensity. We were ahead two games to one and couldn't finish," said Jim McLaughlin. "Many teams would fold after losing a five-game heartbreaker and then playing at Stanford the next day. We learned a great deal against Stanford. We saw that when we play our game to our standards, we can beat any team in the nation. We fell behind to a very good team and found a way to win."

The euphoria of beating Stanford ended after the postgame trip to the Cheesecake Factory. Coming in the next Thursday and Friday were number seven UCLA and number four USC. Could our young team come down from rush of beating Stanford and be ready for the Southern California schools? "We have to start faster and keep our intensity for an entire match. The PAC-10 is too strong to keep playing from behind," said Coach McLaughlin. Well, coach, the team was listening. Aided by nearly six thousand very loud fans, our Huskies swept both UCLA and USC. The wins lifted our Huskies to number four in the nation and increased our home winning streak to thirty-eight.

We now know a great deal about this team. We know that Christal is one of the best ever. Stevie, Jessica, and Tama are making strong statements for All American. They will be joined by Alesha Deesing as her thumb heals. We know that Megan McAfee and Ashley Aratani have ice water in their veins at crunch time, and our freshmen, Jenna, Becky, and Kindra, will be big-time players for the next three years. We know at the halfway point in the PAC-10 season that our Huskies are a good team. Their goal over the next two months is to become a great team.

The team pushed the record home winning streak to thirty-nine matches before losing a five-game heartbreaker to Stanford. The team won four of the next five matches to finish second in the PAC-10 behind Stanford. This was the fourth consecutive PAC-10 season where UW and Stanford finished first or second. Despite the team's 26-3 record going into the NCAA tournament, something seemed to be missing. They seemed flat during the last two matches against Oregon State and Oregon. The first two rounds of the NCAA tournament were in Seattle, so there was reason to be encouraged. UW had never lost a tournament match in Seattle. The first-round match against Missouri was far more difficult than expected. The match went five games before the Huskies could eliminate Missouri. It was a long and very grueling match. The team looked flat and tired, but a win is a win. The next night was BYU, with the winner traveling to Penn State for the Sweet 16. The UW faithful fully expected to be making a trip to Penn State. Penn State was also ready to avenge last year's loss in Seattle.

The Seattle weather sent the first ominous sign when it snowed most of the day. Snow on December 1 is not usual. Driving in Seattle is always a challenge, but driving with snow makes things very treacherous. The weather kept some fans home. Fewer than three thousand people attended the match. BYU drew first blood, winning game one. There was an eerie feeling in the arena. UW won the next two games and was in position to secure the win. BYU won game four handily, setting up the seventh five-game match of the year. All three UW losses were five game matches. With the crowd on its feet as the fifth game began, UW could not break away from the scrappy BYU team. With the score tied at 9-9, BYU strung together three straight points for a 12-9 lead before Washington got to within one at 14-13. But it was not meant to be, as BYU recorded the upset victory. The crowd and the team were stunned. Neither could believe what just happened. This group of seniors had been to three Final Fours. All they knew was the week before Christmas, they were supposed to be playing for a chance to win another national title. "I told these guys this loss is going to hurt, and it's going to hurt for awhile, mostly because of the way that we go about things. They give everything that they have every day," said a disappointment Jim McLaughlin.

As the stunned crowd left the arena, one supporter told me, "We had a great run." I relied, "It's not over yet. We had three freshmen, a sophomore, and a junior playing most of the match. They will learn from this, plus next year we will have more of the right people joining the program." Airial Salvo and Jill Collymore, both redshirts, would join Becky Perry and Kindra Carlson up front. Three very promising incoming freshmen middle blockers, Bianca Rowland, Lauren Barfield, and Kelcey Dunaway, would help Jessica Swarbrick, who would be the only senior. Tama and Megan McAfee would return to the back row. They would be good, but they were so young.

* * *

After the holidays, Jim asked me to come to Seattle and help the coaches' work on updating, modifying, or changing their recruiting plan. He told me, "We need a better mix of youth and experience every year." Then he told me, "Jessica Swarbrick came into my office to talk about next season. She started to cry and said, 'We were better than the 2006 team that went to the Final Four, but we just lost our focus. We didn't do what we knew needed to be done. It was like we felt were entitled to go to the Final Four. I guarantee that won't happen next season.' I told her we are going to be very young again. She is the only senior. Then she told me, 'I will not allow anyone to relax or feel they are doing well enough to get it done. We will get back to the Husky way.'"

"Wow, Jim that is a very powerful statement from someone so young."

"That's why we need to revamp our recruiting model. We simply cannot be so senior heavy like the championship team or so young like this year and next season. We need a better funnel."

With that, Jim scheduled a three-day-off campus meeting to review, modify, and/or update the recruiting procedures.

Even though the program had reached elite status, we were not getting the "top recruit." Programs like Stanford and Penn State seemed to capture the "can't-miss player." These programs just reload each year. UW was the unsuccessful finalist against Stanford and Penn State for several top recruits. These programs are always in the conversation for the national title. Maybe it was their two decades of excellence against Jim's five years. Maybe it was that they had twenty years of building their brand with the junior programs. Maybe it was the weather in Seattle. Maybe it was the ploy opposing coaches used that Jim McLaughlin would leave UW to coach the Olympic team. Maybe they were just better at identifying players sooner in the process.

This is not to say that UW has not attracted excellent players. The UW players are very good. They have the character and discipline to fit into the program. They do what it takes and make themselves the best that they can be. It is a tribute to the UW student/athletes and coaches that this program has achieved such great success. But the fact remains that the "cream of the crop" was not going to Washington.

To make matters more difficult, players were giving verbal commitments as high school sophomores. While a verbal commitment is not binding, more times than not both the player and school honor a verbal commitment. In addition, other schools will back away—"call off the dogs," as Leslie Tuiasosopo says—when a player gives a verbal commitment. This means programs now have to identify and start tracking players while they are still in junior high.

The "Jim McLaughlin is going to leave to coach the Olympic team" story that opposing coaches had been using ended January 18, 2008, when UW signed him to an extension through the 2012 season. The next Olympics would be during the 2012 season.

With that distraction out of the way, we locked ourselves away and completely dissected our recruiting program and processes. The goal was to create a recruiting model that would attract the caliber of athlete that would give UW a legitimate opportunity to win the national title every year. Listed below is a summary of the plan initially developed in January 2008:

Recruiting Plan—Executive Summary

University of Washington (UW) volleyball is one of the elite programs in the nation. Over the past four years, UW has become the best program in the PAC-10. The record speaks for itself:

- Winning Percentage   90%
- Final Four Appearances   3
- National Champions   1
- PAC-10 Titles   2
- All Americans   15
- National Player of the Year   2
- All PAC 10   25
- National Team Members   2
- PAC-10 All Academic   16
- Graduation Rate   100%
- Ave Home Crowd/Match   3,000

Recruiting is the key to sustain this success. UW has implemented this recruiting plan to identify the top student-athletes early in their prep career (fourteen years old) then systematically track and evaluate their progress. The plan will put UW in the strongest position to secure the student/athletes that are the best fit for the program.

- Identification of Recruiting Areas—the identification process is divided into five target areas
- Data Collection Process—build a list per recruiting area
- Ranking Levels—rate recruits into one of seven categories
- Recruit Checklist—the minimum information that must be collected on a recruit
- Recruiting Priority—traits and characteristics
- Monitoring and Evaluation—keeping tabs of potential recruits

- Recruit Review—formal and scheduled meeting to determine next steps
- Contact with Recruits and Coaches—who does what and when
- Unsolicited recruit letter or e-mail management—how and when to add or remove a recruit
- On-campus Visits—plan for official and unofficial visits

We also discussed our donation plan. Since 2006, it appeared we had reached the $35,000 to $40,000 plateau. We discussed the season ticket plan and if football and men's basketball season ticket holders could be given the option to make a donation to volleyball. While we were at the hotel, Jim received a call that the Gettinger family, longtime supporters of all Washington athletic programs, had just created a $200,000 scholarship endowment for the volleyball program. This was tremendous news and another example of the love and generosity the people of Seattle have for the University of Washington.

We knew we had made a significant improvement in our recruiting model. Each year would bring more tuning to the model. How successful will the plan be? Only time will tell. The freshmen entering in 2009, 2010, 2011, and beyond will determine the success.

Chapter 13

THE HEDGEHOG CONCEPT—KEEP IT SIMPLE

* * *

Earlier we mentioned something called the Hedgehog Concept from Jim Collins' book *Good to Great*. In the book, Mr. Collins describes the famous essay "The Hedgehog and the Fox," by Isaiah Berlin. Mr. Berlin divided the world into hedgehogs and foxes based on an ancient Greek parable. Mr. Collins writes:

> The fox is a cunning creature, able to devise a myriad of complex strategies for sneak attacks upon the hedgehog…The hedgehog is a dowdier creature…spends his day searching for lunch and taking care of his home.
>
> The fox plots and plans a complex series of daily attacks, while the hedgehog focuses solely on what it deems important. When the fox leaps out to attack, the hedgehog simply rolls into a perfect little ball. It becomes a sphere of sharp spikes, pointing outward in all directions. The fox is forced to retreat and continues to plan and plot its next failure.

I have met and known many executives and businesses that were like the fox. They pursued too many options and alternatives. They dabbled in too many activities and stretched both the revenue and manpower far too thin. As Mr. Berlin states in *Good to Great*, "The fox never integrates their thinking into one overall concept or unifying vision." These types of businesses may find some degree of success, but will never excel; never become great.

Since I did turn-arounds of failing companies, I was often called in to fix the scattered actions created by the fox. I had to be more like the hedgehog. The businesses simply did not have the funds to continue as a fox. Again, Mr. Collins writes:

It doesn't matter how complex the world, a hedgehog reduces all challenges and dilemmas to simple—indeed almost simplistic—hedgehog ideas. For the hedgehog, anything that does not somehow relate to the hedgehog idea holds no relevance.

For me this meant find out what we can do best and do it better than everyone else. It is basically the KISS model— "Keep It Simple, Stupid!" The challenge is not doing what you are doing better; it is discovering what you can become the best at. Once again, I defer to Mr. Collins:

A Hedgehog Concept is not a goal to be the best, a strategy to be the best, an intention to be the best, a plan to be the best. It is an *understanding* of what you *can* be the best at. The distinction is absolutely critical.

I take this to mean that the business or organization may have to change not only how it does business, but what business it actually does. This type of change does not occur overnight. It takes time to implement the Ten Turn-Around Rules. This is not a simple thing. It takes courage, confidence, a single-minded purpose, and, most of all, a total and complete passion to do what it takes to make it happen.

* * *

For UW volleyball, the 2008 season was returning to its Hedgehog Concept. The team was so young that teaching and coaching went back to the basic fundamentals. The message was loud and clear: "There are no small things in volleyball." Players and coaches watched more video of practices and training than ever before. Once again the preseason poll experts did not give the program much love. The team was ranked fifth in the PAC-10 and eighth in the nation. Fifth in the PAC-10; I couldn't believe it. If the team needed any additional motivation, being ranked fifth in the PAC-10 was that motivation.

As always, the team started the season strong, going 7-0, but dropped from number eight to number nine in the polls. The first loss was a five-game heartbreaker to Hawaii in Hawaii, which dropped the team to number ten in the polls. The PAC-10 season opened with two five-game wins against the Arizona schools. This was followed by back-to-back 3-0 losses to Cal and Stanford at home. Back-to-back losses at home! It seemed like forever since that happened. "We hit the ball out a lot, which is a function of composure," said head coach Jim McLaughlin. "We have to have better composure out there. We've got to take good swings and play aggressively. We have a lot of things to work on. We've got to learn from this and develop tough swings and make the right choices."

The schedule didn't get easier. Next up were USC and UCLA on the road. In watching these matches, there appeared to be an awakening or an epiphany for the young Huskies. They battled back from adversity and defeated both UCLA and USC 3-2. They won the next three matches and found themselves ranked number six as they headed to the Bay Area for the rematch with Stanford and Cal. Stanford won 3-0, but the young team showed they were learning composure as they beat Cal 3-0. "We kept pressure on them start to finish," said McLaughlin. "We did a nice job on defense and touched almost every ball. We played well. I thought it complemented what we did in practice last week, which the Stanford match didn't. Any time a game complements what you did in practice, it's the best thing in coaching."

Maybe this young collection of players was finding its stride. Senior All American Jessica Swarbrick was relentless. She was on pace to break the all-time hitting percentage record. She was on pace to hit over .400 for her career. This is remarkable given her setter the last two years was a freshman and sophomore. Jessica became like Courtney Thompson. She just willed her team to win. She also imposed an extremely high standard of behavior both on the court and in the team room. I was told by one of the freshmen that before one match, Jessica entered the team room to find the music blaring and some of the underclassmen dancing. "It looked like fire shot out of her eyes, and she let us know in

very descriptive and graphic terms that our actions were 'unac-
ceptable'. Everyone straightened up in a heartbeat. No one on
the team wanted to disappoint Jessy, and we certainly did not
want to incur her wrath. I have never seen anyone so focused
and committed."

The Huskies moved up to number five after the Cal sweep.
They ended the PAC-10 season with eight consecutive wins
and finished second in the PAC-10, not fifth as the experts had
predicted. The team was peaking at the right time. The first
two rounds of the NCAA Tournament were in Seattle. The team
wanted to avenge last year's second-round home loss. "It's a
good way to finish the PAC-10, and now the best part of the year
starts," said McLaughlin. "We've got to approach it like it's the
last match of the season, which it could be. We can't worry about
the next one, we can't worry about our record, our seed, or our
wins. Nothing matters but our preparation and focus."

UW entered the tournament with a 25-4 record. Big Sky
champion Portland State was the first-round opponent. The Huskies won 3-0 in one hour. I leaned over to my youngest daughter
and whispered, "This is how a PAC-10 team is supposed to play
against a Big Sky team." Next up was Santa Clara who was also
swept in about one hour. Utah, Michigan, and Nebraska arrived
in Seattle for the regional finals. If things went as expected, UW
and Nebraska would meet, with the winner advancing to the
Final Four.

The first step, however, was to beat Utah. There was some
additional drama to this match. Junior Airial Salvo had transferred from Utah to UW. Her setter at Utah, Sydney Anderson,
had transferred to Nebraska. Both requests to be released from
their scholarships were denied. This meant Airial and Sydney
had to sit out last year. I don't know how sitting out affected
Sydney, but I do know it did not make Airial a happy camper.
Leading up to the match, I asked her mother, Lori, how Airial
was doing. Her mom said, "She is trying to keep it all in perspec-
tive and treat it like any other match. Stay within herself and
her game." Then I asked her mother how she was feeling. Her
response: "I was doing pretty well until I heard the Utah coach

made a comment that 'we are going to show them they went to the wrong school.' Now I want us to kick their ass!" UW swept Utah 3-0. Airial must have heard her mother. Facing her former team, Airial had one of her best nights in the Purple and Gold. She hit a season-high .483, her best hitting efficiency as a Husky, with a match-high fifteen kills on twenty-nine attacks with just one error. "This wasn't about me against Utah," said Airial after the match. "It was about UW getting to the regional championship." She said all the right things, but deep down inside, I knew she felt vindicated.

Up next was Nebraska. The "Big Red" had been hoping for a rematch with UW since losing the 2005 national championship. The problem was Nebraska was not playing the 2005 national champions. That match was history. Still, Nebraska wanted this win desperately, since the Final Four the following week was back in Omaha. The atmosphere in the arena was electric. Over five thousand UW faithful came to see what they hoped would be the fourth trip to the Final Four in five years. Things started our great with UW winning the first two games. It seemed like déjà vu all over again. At the break I could hear people starting to make airline and hotel reservations to Omaha.

Nebraska came out focused and easily won game three. The fourth game was a classic. Nebraska used runs of five and four points to go up 18-11. The Huskies refused to die and continued to chip away at the Nebraska lead. Down 22-15, a hard kill by Jessica Swarbrick touched off a six-point Husky rally that included four straight kills by Airial Salvo to bring the Huskies back within a point, 22-21, forcing Nebraska into its second timeout. The teams tied at 23-23, but a Washington service error put Nebraska up by one. Washington tied it on a kill by Airial Salvo, 24-24. Nebraska ended the game on a kill and a service ace to take the game in extra points, 26-24. This game had heart-pounding action with the entire crowd standing and screaming throughout. The berth in the Final Four was coming down to a fifteen-point fifth game. Washington came out hot, taking the first three points, forcing Nebraska into its first timeout. A Washington service error put Nebraska on the board, but UW took three more on a kill by Airial Salvo, a kill by Jessica Swarbrick, and a block by Jenna Hagglund, putting UW up, 6-1. Nebraska took two points back, but three straight errors gave Washington a strong 9-3 advantage. Nebraska called its second timeout. Washington found itself in a difficult rotation, and Nebraska reeled off nine straight points to take a 12-9 lead. Back-to-back kills by Jill Collymore and Airial Salvo put Washington within a point, 12-11. Nebraska came up with a block to go up 13-11, but the Huskies forced an error to get within a point again, 13-12. A huge block by Kindra Carlson and Jessica Swarbrick tied the set at 13-13 and gave the Huskies another shot, but a Washington attack error and a short Nebraska service ace shut the door on the Huskies' rally.

I had never experience a match with so much excitement and emotion. The crowd stood and applauded both teams for five minutes. This contest was as good as it gets. Unlike last year's loss, the crowd was not stunned. Every Husky fan felt terrible for this young team. They had come so close to the Promised Land when no one had given them a chance. The heart of everyone in the arena went out to Jessica Swarbrick. The lone senior had given every ounce of effort to lead her team to this position. The young woman who cried in Jim McLaughlin's office and guaranteed the 2008 team would do things the right way had made good on her promise. Each player had tears in her eyes as she left the locker room. Each was consoled by her parents and family. Each player said how sad she was for Jessica. When Jessica came out, she was sad that her career had ended without another trip to the Final Four, but she had a look of satisfaction that she had done all she could to elevate this team to within two points of the Final Four.

"It's a tough thing to deal with right now," said Jim McLaughlin of the loss. "It will probably be tough for a while. We played well at times, but Nebraska did what they had to do and they won the thing. It's hard when you lose games like this, but sometimes what makes it so hard is what ends up making it so great. It's just hard right now." When I heard this at the press conference, all I could think about was Tom Hanks line to Geena Davis in the movie *A League of Their Own*. Geena Davis is about to drive home with her husband. She had just said, "It just got too hard." Tom Hanks line was, "It's supposed to be hard. If it wasn't, everyone would do it. It's the hard that makes it great."

* * *

After the 2008 season, our donations were again about $40,000. We all knew that 2009 was going to bring the worst recession we had ever seen in our adult lives. We knew every business and every person was going to eliminate any expense that was not absolutely necessary. We knew that during difficult economic times, donations to athletic programs often suffered. I had the good fortune to speak at the volleyball banquet in January 2009. My talk is reprinted below:

TWO Points from the Final Four

Think back to the August preseason polls—the experts picked our Huskies to finish fifth in PAC-10 and number eight in the nation. The word was the Huskies had lost too much over the past few years; they were too young and untested at the outside and setter positions; they were starting a true freshman in the middle; even returning All-Americans Jessica Swarbrick and Tama Miyashiro and the great Jim McLaughlin's coaching weren't going to be enough this time. We even heard PAC-10 coaches whispering that this was the year they could exact some revenge on the Huskies. Well, at the end of the season, our Huskies were two points away from their fourth Final Four in five years. We were treated to another tremendous volleyball season.

Now comes the challenge for us—the Husky fans and donors. The economic situation is going to force some very difficult decisions. As a business owner, there are investments that I will have to cut back or cut out completely. Many of you will be doing the same. As business owners and investors, we look at four key criteria over a minimum of five years before we invest.

1. Record/Performance—how does this entity perform in the market;
2. Rank vs. comparable businesses;
3. Management;
4. Product demand now and in the future.

Record/Performance—Over the past five years, Husky volleyball has been successful 89 percent of the time. I own an insurance agency. We are thrilled if we win one out of three. How many of your investments are successful nine out of ten times?

Rank vs. comparable businesses—If an investment can be in the top 5 percent in its industry, it is considered a top performer. Over the past five years Husky volleyball's average national ranking is number four. Given there are 330-plus Division 1 colleges that play volleyball, which puts them in the top 1.5 percent in their industry.

Management—Strong stable management is the key to continuous and long-term success. Jim McLaughlin is the best volleyball coach in the world, period. **Enough said.**

Product demand now and in the future—The product is the student-athletes, who are among the best in the nation. Given that volleyball is second only to soccer in worldwide growth and participation, there will be more and better student-athletes coming to UW.

Arrogance often develops when a business experiences great success over a long period of time. We start to see an attitude of entitlement. Did you follow the "bailout" debates? I have not seen any arrogance with this program. In fact, after the last match, each player left the locker room with tears in her eyes. They felt as if somehow they had let us down. Can you believe that? They give us another tremendous season and they feel they let us down. I walked over to the two tables where the players were seated and said to them, "Ladies, I speak for the nearly fifty thousand people that watched you play this year; you have never let us down! Never!"

I walked toward the fans and donors who were seated behind the team and said, "When was the last time one of your investments apologized to you for winning 89 percent of the time; was in the top 1.5 percent; had the best management and product/employees?"

As a business owner and investor, if I can find one employee or one investment opportunity that has the results and the management like Husky volleyball and had people who cared as much as these young women, I will not only continue to invest, but I will increase the amount.

The program needs our help. Their goal is the Final Four and another national title—but they can't do it alone. I can tell you from firsthand experience, there is nothing like the elation, the total and complete "throw your head back and thrust your hands in the air *thank you, God!*" elation I felt when our Huskies won the national title in San Antonio. It is going to happen again, and I want you all to be there and experience it yourself. It is something you will treasure forever.

Many times our best investments are in the development of young people, because we get to share their journey. They gave all they had for us—let's do the same. If you haven't joined POINT! HUSKIES!, do it. Do it today! Make a donation. Give what you can. Be part of the celebration that is Husky volleyball."

I left the banquet hoping for the best but fearing the worst.

✻ ✻ ✻

In the off-season we worked on two projects:

- time management and delegation
- reaching out to the volleyball alumni

The coaches were spending twelve to fourteen hours working during the off-season. Sometimes it is easier to get to the top than to stay on top. We listed all functions and tasks performed by each coach. Once they were defined, we prioritized each task. The goal was to accomplish the high-priority functions as efficiently as possible. I recall saying, "There is simply not enough time in the day to accomplish everything, so we need to focus on the important things." People burn out when they feel it is impossible to do all that needs to be done.

I told the coaches about a situation I had with one of my turn-around jobs. Each executive had an administrative assistant and many of the assistants had an assistant. Everyone was busy all the time doing busywork. Much of what was being done had nothing to do with generating revenue or increasing profit or increasing market share or increasing customer satisfaction. Things were being done because they were always done. No one ever asked why. My division had one administrative assistant. She constantly complained to me that the other assistants had people to help them. She told me, "There are things I can't get done without some help." I asked her, "Like what?"

"Like the color charts and graphs the other executives use at the managers' meeting."

I asked her, "Have I ever asked you for color charts and graphs?" "No," was the reply.

"Do you know why?" I asked. Again the answer was, "No."

"The reason why is because they aren't important. I only have one assistant because it forces us to focus on defining and accomplishing what is important. All the other stuff looks good but doesn't accomplish anything of real value."

The time management program appeared to work. The coaches were able to see their families in the off-season.

The second task was to reconnect with the volleyball alumni. Some of the former players felt left out. These were the players that started the program and kept it going during the early and very lean years. These were the players who had the terrible practice times, little to no access to trainers, wore uniforms made by the coaches' wives, travelled on rickety old buses, but kept the dream alive. They were happy the program had reached elite status but wished they could have some type of involvement.

The first function was to have a cocktail party prior to the UCLA match. We had an excellent turnout. Over 250 former players, spouses, children, and donors attended. A large number of the 2005 championship team also attended. I went to every table to meet and talk with every former player and hear some of their stories. They all seemed happy to see each other and be recognized by the program. I gave the following short talk before the match began.

"Coach McLaughlin is getting the team ready but he wanted me to thank you all for coming tonight. I want to start off by giving you some information. I spoke at the volleyball banquet last January and thanked all the donors for contributing a record amount of $42,000. We talked about this terrible recession and the impact it would have on everything and everyone. We talked about the volleyball program as an investment rather than a donation. We talked about how fortunate we are to be actively involved with this investment. I left the banquet hoping for the best but preparing for the worst. Today I learned from the Tyee office that despite this terrible recession, you invested a record $60,000 to this program. This far exceeds our wildest expectations. Of course you know, as this recessions ends, I will be expecting more than $60,000. Give yourselves a hand." This brought both laughter and applause.

"To the pre-Jim players, we cannot thank you enough for keeping this program going. After some of the stories

I heard here tonight, I am amazed you stayed with the program. Without your dedication and commitment during the early days of Title IX, this program would have ended years ago. Had it not been for you, we would not have the great success of the past few years. You made it possible for today's players to have these great facilities. You made it possible for there to be a national championship team.

"To the '05 team, it is wonderful to see so many of you here. You accomplished what every program in the nation *wishes* it could do. You brought home the first national title. There will be more, hopefully this year, but you were the first. The '05 team will forever be the 'gold standard' for Husky volleyball.

"Again, thank you all for coming, and enjoy tonight's match."

There were lots of hugs and exchanging of e-mail addresses and phone numbers. All of the alumni were honored at the break. The connection had begun.

In the spring of 2010, the program hosted an alumni game and dinner. Members of the current team were at each table and introduced the alumni at their table. Both the current and former players enjoyed the day, and plans are under way for the next alumni game.

The Hedgehog Concept was alive and well.

Chapter 14

SUMMARY—MISSION ACCOMPLISHED

* * *

As I reflect on the UW volleyball program from 2001 to today, it gives me a tremendous sense of pride and satisfaction. This program at this great university had hit rock bottom. Other than parents and family, there was not much interest or hope for better times. Donations were basically nonexistent. The alumni, even though the large majority still lived in Seattle, rarely returned. It was a sad situation. The first time I saw UW play volleyball at Sacramento State, I wondered if the turn-around rules that I used with businesses could work with an athletic program.

Fortunately Barbara Hedges knew a guy, and that guy, Jim McLaughlin, had a plan. From our very first meeting, I believed in Jim McLaughlin, and together we devised a plan to turn this program around. Jim coached the team and I worked the business plan. So the question is this: did the turn-around rules listed in the book actually work? Let's take a look.

1. **Everything starts with having the right leader.** This is a no-brainer. Jim McLaughlin's record speaks for itself.
2. **The leader must clearly articulate his or her vision.** The vision has been clear since day one.

   - *Graduate every player*—done.
   - *Finish in the top three in the PAC-10 every year. This gives the team the opportunity to compete for the national title*—finished first or second in the PAC-10 every year since 2004.
   - *Prepare players for the U.S. national team*—Courtney Thompson, Christal Morrison, Candace Lee, Jill Collymore, and Tamari Miyashiro have all played on the

national team. In addition, Sanja Tomasevic, Allison Richardson, Stevie Mussie, Courtney Thompson, Christal Morrison, Darla Myhre, Jessica Swarbrick, Alesha Deesing, and Airial Salvo have all played professionally.

3. **The leader must inspire people to believe.** Ask any of the nearly three thousand people who attend every UW volleyball home match if they believe. Ask the NCAA Final Four selection committee, who awarded Seattle and UW the host school position for the Final Four in 2013. A city does not host the finals unless it has developed an extremely large and loyal group of believers.

4. **The leader must clearly define what he or she wants to do and what pieces he or she needs to get there.** Going from last place to national champions in four years addresses this rule.

5. **The leader must select the right people and put them in the best position to succeed.** Jim has shown the courage to select people who buy into the program and move them into roles that they didn't think were possible.

6. **The leader must focus on the details and training. Make sure everyone knows not only what to do, but how and why to do it.** Watch one UW practice or attend one team meeting and you will witness this first hand.

7. **The leader must insist that everything is documented. The organization must be able to operate without key people present**. The documentation is obvious by walking into Jim's office or the team room. The fact is, the program has survived major injuries to All American players and continued to excel.

8. **The leader must constantly review all aspects of the operation and make adjustments as needed to stay on course.** Changing assistant coaches after going to the Final Four; moving Sanja to a new position to win the National Title; changing the recruiting plan.

9. **The leader must continue to bring in people that are better than the ones already in place**. Elite players are now enrolling and committing to UW.

10. **The leader cannot lose sight of the goal**. Eight straight NCAA appearance; five trips to the Elite 8; three consecutive Final Fours; one national title. This program is now in the national championship conversation every year. More PAC-10 and national championships are coming.

I think we can safely say that the turn-around rules are not limited to for-profit businesses. With the right leader, the rules can be applied to any type or size of business or organization. So if your business or organization is at a cross roads give these rules a try. They are not easy. They will test and challenge you in ways you could never imagine, but in the end they work. Give me a call. I will be happy to help where I can.

Then, when you get a break in your schedule, do yourself a favor and go see the University of Washington volleyball team play. You won't be sorry. Plan a trip to Seattle for the Final Four the week before Christmas in 2013. There is a good chance the University of Washington team will there. Go Huskies!

Made in the USA
Lexington, KY
09 December 2010